HOW TO
SHAPE UP
YOUR HEALTH

"Enjoy good health."
—3 JOHN 2

STAN TOLER

wesleyan
publishing
house

Indianapolis, Indiana

CONTENTS

EAT WELL

RECOMMENDED READING

Total Quality Life, chapter 4, pages 53–58

Christians are disciples of Jesus Christ. The word *disciple* is related to the word *discipline*. You cannot be a disciple without being disciplined. I consider myself a fairly disciplined person. I am a self-starter and have never needed anyone looking over my shoulder to make sure I was doing what I was supposed to be doing. One area where many people struggle to remain disciplined once they reach adulthood, however, is with their health. For many in my generation, the first two decades were the most active years of our lives. As a result, we didn't concern ourselves much with our health and rarely worried about what or how much we ate. We didn't concern ourselves much with our weight, and we stayed in pretty good shape for the most part.

Once we reach adulthood, however, it is generally more difficult to stay active, and we have to start watching what we eat more carefully. Over the next six weeks, as we apply total quality life to our health, I want you to know we are all in the same boat. Maintaining physical fitness is a daily battle, and some days it is more of a struggle than others. When we experience victory in this battle, we achieve not only greater health, but greater satisfaction. Taking care of my health will make me a better husband, father, pastor, teacher, and friend; so I keep fighting.

To assist in obtaining better health, I am offering a health tip at the end of each day. Most of these tips are common sense. However, please note that these tips are in no way medical advice; they are simply suggestions. As always, check with your doctor before beginning anything new.

Total quality health starts with watching what we eat. We must eat well to live well.

DAY 1

~⚜~

DEUTERONOMY 14:1–21

Have you ever wondered about all those dietary restrictions God gave the Israelites back in the Old Testament? Why would he include such seemingly trivial things in his covenant with his people? What was the logic behind some animals being declared clean and others unclean?

Scholars usually offer one of four explanations for these dietary prohibitions. First, the restrictions might have been given for practical, hygienic reasons. In ancient times, some animals carried greater risks of diseases than others, so, following the dietary laws would probably have been better for a person's overall health. Another possible explanation is that these particular animals were declared off-limits because they were commonly associated with pagan worship and sacrifices. A third attempt to explain the prohibitions is that the clean and unclean animals were meant to symbolize good and evil. Finally, some think the lists may have been purely arbitrary on God's part, representing nothing more than God's desire that his children be different from the rest of society.

There is no way to know for sure which, if any, of these views is correct. The only hint of a reason the Bible gives is found in verse 21: "You are a people holy to the LORD your God." That statement is a summary of an earlier explanation about another restriction: "You are a people holy to the LORD your God. Out of all the peoples on the face of the earth, the LORD has chosen you to be his treasured possession" (v. 2). That explanation—that he was Israel's covenant God—was all God deemed necessary.

Many years later, Jesus declared all foods clean (Mark 7:19), and Peter had a vision that convinced him that the ancient dietary laws were no longer required by God (Acts 10:9–23). As a result, most Christians today don't follow these rules. Still, under God's new covenant, those who follow Jesus are God's "chosen people," and we are urged to live holy lives (1 Pet. 2:9–12). So, even though Christians are free from any specific rules or laws regarding our diet, we should not take this to mean that God is unconcerned about what or how we eat. Always remember and live by the words of the apostle Paul: "Whether you eat or drink or whatever you do, do it all for the glory of God" (1 Cor. 10:31).

DAILY HEALTH TIP

Add whole grain to your diet. The main benefit of a diet high in whole grain foods is a reduced risk of developing cardiovascular diseases. Examples of whole grain foods include: popcorn, brown rice, wild rice, oatmeal, and wheat.

QUESTIONS FOR REFLECTION

1. On a scale of one to ten (one being poor and ten being excellent), how would you rank your overall health? Why did you answer the way you did? What changes would you like to see in your life over the next six weeks?

2. What do you think of the four possible explanations given as to why God placed restrictions on the Israelites' diet? Which explanation do you think is the best? Why?

3. As a Christian, how should your attitude about dieting, eating, and being healthy, be different from a non-Christian?

PRAYER FOR TODAY

Lord, thank you for delivering me by your grace from the curse of the law and for choosing me to be your treasured possession. I want to glorify you in everything I do—even in what I eat and drink. Give me the resolve, focus, and discipline necessary to practice healthy eating habits. In the strong name of Jesus I pray. Amen.

DAY 2

GENESIS 3:1–19

On the sixth day of creation, God created humanity. He created man and woman in his image and likeness and said to them, "I give you every seed-bearing plant on the face of the whole earth and every tree that has fruit with seed in it. They will be yours for food. And to all the beasts of the earth and all the birds of the air and all the creatures that move on the ground—everything that has the breath of life in it—I give every green plant for food. And it was so" (Gen. 1:29–30). In the beginning, God said all food was good, but later he placed restrictions on what his people could eat, and today many of the things we eat could not be considered good food. So, what happened?

Sometime after creation—we are not told when or how long—Adam and Eve were enjoying a blissful existence in the garden, when a beautiful, crafty serpent convinced Eve to eat a certain piece of fruit that God had forbidden. The Hebrew word does not specify what kind of fruit; it is the more general term for any kind of fruit. So why do many people assume it was an apple? It all started in the fourth century when the Bible was translated into Latin. The serpent told Eve that once she ate the fruit, she would know "good and evil" (3:5). The Latin word for *evil* happens to be the same as the Latin word for *apple* (*malum*). As a result, people started associating the apple with the fruit Adam and Eve ate in the garden.

Because of the rebellion in the garden, God pronounced a judgment on the serpent (vv. 14–15), the woman (v. 16), the man (v. 17), and even creation itself. Of creation, God said, "Cursed is the ground because of you; through painful toil you will eat of it. . . . It will produce thorns and thistles for you. . . . By the sweat of your brow you will eat your food" (vv. 17–19).

Perhaps it was this part of the curse on creation that included the risks associated with certain types of food. What we can say for certain though, is that Adam and Eve's inability to overcome the temptations related to food is one that most of their descendants have wrestled with at one time or another. Sometimes this is because we eat to excess, rather than in moderation. Sometimes it is because we fill up on junk foods and highly processed foods rather than sticking with nature's nutrition. The good news is that God can give you both the desire and the power to resist temptation.

DAILY HEALTH TIP

Eat your vegetables, especially those that are fresh and in-season. Vegetables contain antioxidants that may help fight off certain cancers, as well as prevent heart disease and strokes. The well-worn guideline is still good advice: eat something green at every meal.

QUESTIONS FOR REFLECTION

1. What are some foods you eat that you know are bad for you? Why do you eat them?

2. Read Romans 8:19–21. What do you think Paul meant when he wrote, "Creation itself will be liberated from its bondage"? How do you think this applies to planting and harvesting?

3. How do you think God's redemption of our lives impacts our ability to live a healthy lifestyle?

PRAYER FOR TODAY

Father God, thank you for loving me unconditionally, for creating me in your image, and for providing for my redemption. Guide my every thought and action so that every choice I make—even in my food and drink—returns glory to you. In Jesus' wonderful name I pray. Amen.

DAY 3

PROVERBS 23:1–3, 19–21

The Bible gives plenty of room for us to enjoy the blessings of God's creation, including the delicious tastes of a skillfully prepared, nutritious meal. But the Bible also issues some strong warnings about overeating.

Near the end of the sixth century A.D., church leaders began to notice that most sins could be categorized under seven headings. Those seven headings became known as the seven deadly sins, and it was believed that all the evils in the world were rooted in these seven deadly sins: laziness (sloth), lust, anger, pride, envy, gluttony, and greed. Many church leaders have considered gluttony to be the deadliest of the deadly sins.

Proverbs warns us not to gorge ourselves on too much food, especially if we are an invited guest in someone's house. Proverbs also warns us to control our appetites because the person feeding us may be fattening us up for their own purposes (vv. 1–3). Gluttony is associated with excess in other areas, like drunkenness, and can lead a person to a life of poverty. However, the person who can control their appetite is considered wise (vv. 19–21).

Many are fortunate enough to live in an affluent society, but our abundance of food and drink has led in turn to an abundance of eating disorders—from obesity to bulimia to anorexia. We eat not just for daily sustenance or when we are hungry, but to hide our emotions, celebrate important events, close a business deal, or try and kill the pain of depression and loneliness. Those who are wise learn to say no, resist, and back away from the table, or, in the words of the writer of Proverbs, to "put a knife to [their] throat[s]" (v. 2) instead of to the meat. Don't take that verse literally; the writer was merely emphasizing the deceptive temptation to overindulge and the critical nature of controlling our appetites. In contrast, the way of wisdom is to learn to be satisfied with what our bodies need.

DAILY HEALTH TIP

Fruit makes a wonderful snack. Begin the practice of always having a bowl of fruit in your house. People who eat a lot of fruit are less likely to develop diabetes, Alzheimer's, and cancer. Fruit also provides your body with nutrients to fight off other infections, as well as to repair cells.

QUESTIONS FOR REFLECTION

1. How would you define gluttony? Why do you think church leaders considered gluttony to be the deadliest of sins? Do you agree with their assessment? Why or why not?

2. How do you think healthy eating habits can be an indication of one's desire to honor God?

PRAYER FOR TODAY

Heavenly Father, sanctify my life not only in word, but also in deed and behavior. Grant me the grace of self-control and help me to resist the temptation of overindulging in your good gifts. In the powerful name of Jesus. Amen.

DAY 4

DANIEL 1:1–21

Have you ever told a friend about a horrible dream you had the night before, and the first response from your friend was, "What did you eat last night?" We know instinctively that there is a relationship between what we eat and how well we sleep. We also know there is a relationship between what we eat and how much energy we have and how productive we are at work. Eating right makes a huge difference in our lives.

In the ancient world, when one nation conquered another, it was common for the victorious nation to claim the most gifted and talented young people from the conquered nation and educate them in the wisdom and customs of the conquering nation. This is precisely what happened to Daniel and his three friends Hananiah (Shadrach), Mishael (Meshach), and Azariah (Abednego) when the kingdom of Babylon went to war against the declining kingdom of Judah.

Daniel and his friends were deported to Babylon and suddenly found themselves in a privileged situation. They received specialized training and were provided food and drink from the king's table. "But Daniel resolved not to defile himself with the royal food and wine" (v. 8). It seems the royal diet did not square with the dietary guidelines in God's law, so Daniel refused to indulge in the sumptuous fare.

The official responsible for Daniel already thought well of him, so when Daniel requested a different diet for himself and his friends, the official granted the request. Their "special" diet consisted entirely of fresh vegetables and water. After ten days, the official noticed that

Daniel and his friends appeared healthier than those who were eating from the king's table, so he agreed to let them continue their diet. We can assume that Daniel and his friends were also more productive and energetic than the others because the official proceeded to put every one of the deported young men on Daniel's diet of vegetables and water.

Daniel was granted health and success because he was obedient to God even in matters of food and drink. God grant us the wisdom and courage to honor God in such things as well!

DAILY HEALTH TIP

Don't forget your protein, and lean protein is the best. Eat more fish, but not fried fish. Salmon and trout are excellent sources of protein. Don't skip breakfast either; eggs and milk are excellent sources of protein. Finally, skin your chicken before cooking and try to avoid processed meats.

QUESTIONS FOR REFLECTION

1. In what ways can the food you eat make a difference in how productive you are during your waking hours and the quality of sleep you get at night?

2. Can you think of ways in which you have "defiled" yourself by what you have eaten?

PRAYER FOR TODAY

Dear Lord, thank you for Daniel's example. Please help me to have a similar fortitude and resolve not to harm myself by what I eat. Instead, help me to follow a diet that will keep me healthy and productive in your kingdom. In Jesus' name. Amen.

DAY 5

As important as it is to eat right, it is even more important to nourish your soul, and the only person who can truly nourish your soul is Jesus Christ. He is the "bread of life" (v. 35).

Many people followed Jesus not because of who he was, but of what he could do for them. Jesus said there were those who followed him "because [they] ate the loaves and had [their] fill" (v. 26). Previously, Jesus had fed five thousand men, women, and children with five loaves and two small fish (6:1–15). He then told the crowd, "Do not work for food that spoils, but for food that endures to eternal life" (v. 27). Who wouldn't want food that lasts for eternity, so the people said to Jesus, "Give us this bread" (v. 34). Jesus responded, "I am the bread of life. He who comes to me will never go hungry" (v. 35).

Jesus is the bread that never goes bad, never decays, and satisfies for all eternity.

In this passage, Jesus drew a simple comparison between himself and the manna God provided the Israelites in the wilderness: one is eternal and the other was temporary. Jesus said, "Your forefathers ate manna and died, but he who feeds on this bread will live forever" (v. 58). And just in case they misunderstood, Jesus spoke even more graphically: "I tell you the truth, unless you eat the flesh of the Son of Man and drink his blood, you have no life in you. Whoever eats my flesh and drinks my blood has eternal life. . . . For my flesh is real food and my blood is real drink. Whoever eats my flesh and drinks my blood remains in me, and I in him" (vv. 53–56). Pretty obvious isn't it? Unless you, by faith, participate with Jesus in his death, you do not have eternal life.

A person can eat all the right foods and be in perfect physical shape and still die. The benefits of a healthy diet are for this life and they are extremely important, but in order to live forever, a person must taste the Bread of Life, Jesus himself.

We have spent this week discussing the need to eat right and maintain a healthy balance. In no way do I mean for this last day to undermine anything that has already been said. It is extremely important to eat well so you can be more productive, happier, and healthier. And the habits that lead to health in this life are habits that will serve you well in God's kingdom. But physical health is worth little if you don't place your faith in Jesus Christ, asking him to feed your soul. Have you done so? Have you placed your faith in the Bread of Life?

DAILY HEALTH TIP

Make sure your diet is low in fat. As much as possible, avoid fats such as butter, saturated fats, animal fats, and dairy fats. Furthermore, avoid fast food restaurants. A low-fat diet is one of the primary keys to keeping your heart healthy.

QUESTIONS FOR REFLECTION

1. What do you think Jesus meant when he described himself as the "bread of life" (v. 35)? How would you explain what he meant to someone else?

2. "What good is it for a man to gain the whole world, yet forfeit his soul?" (Mark 8:36).

PRAYER FOR TODAY

Dear Jesus, thank you for offering yourself as the Bread of Life. Today and every day, I place my faith and trust in you. Sanctify my heart and life for your service by your love, mercy, and grace. In your name I pray. Amen.

WEEK 2
EXERCISE

RECOMMENDED READING

Total Quality Life, chapter 4, pages 60–61; chapter 8, pages 140–146

Exercise is important for everyone, but if your job requires more mental than physical work, exercise is a must. Something as simple as a brisk walk, or some other form of exercise, gets the blood flowing to your brain. Extra blood flow refreshes your mind. Exercise also releases chemicals (endorphins) into your blood stream. These chemicals give you a sense of satisfaction that positively affect your overall attitude and sense of well-being.

Total quality life involves taking care of your health, and a huge part of living a healthy lifestyle is exercise.

DAY 1

1 CORINTHIANS 9:24–27

The two greatest sporting events of New Testament times, the Olympic and Isthmian Games, both climaxed with a marathon race.

The Greek word translated *race* (v. 24) is *stadion*, the root for our English word *stadium*. Paul painted a word picture of marathon runners entering a stadium for the final leg of the great race. Paul said that all runners who compete in the marathon race endure a disciplined training regimen (v. 25).

You may never plan to run a marathon race, but staying in shape so you can live a total quality life still requires that you go through the agony of disciplining yourself, getting off the couch or out of bed to exercise.

But here is the thing to remember: While keeping in shape and exercising regularly is important for living a life of quality, even more important is keeping in shape spiritually. And the more you exercise physically the more energy you will have to exercise spiritually. Both physical and spiritual exercise go together.

DAILY HEALTH TIP

If you are going to start a new exercise program and you have not exercised in a significant amount of time, the most important tip is to start slowly. Gradually build up your speed, strength, and endurance. Starting too fast will set you up for failure.

QUESTIONS FOR REFLECTION

1. Approximately how much physical activity do you get each day at work? Is your job more physical or mental? What can you do this week to become more active?

2. How do you think physical exercise can benefit you, not only physically, but also spiritually? Have you ever considered the connection between physical exercise and spiritual growth?

PRAYER FOR TODAY

Heavenly Father, thank you for the gift of life in the body and for the ability to improve my physical health. As I exercise, please strengthen my body and consecrate it for use in your kingdom. In the name of Jesus I pray. Amen.

DAY 2

❧

PHILIPPIANS 3:12–14

What does your exercise program look like? Did you exercise yesterday? What about today? One of the secrets to keeping an exercise program is accountability. Find someone who can exercise with you, or who can at least hold you accountable. Join an exercise group or a cycling class. In *Total Quality Life*, it says, "Accountability is a way to help us from straying too far from our objectives. Knowing we have to answer to someone for our actions can sometimes make the difference between a good and a bad choice" (p. 140).

Making yourself accountable to someone is what keeps you going when you would rather quit. The apostle Paul knew the importance of accountability, and he knew the importance of pressing on when the going got tough.

Paul's desire was to know Christ in a deep, personal way (Phil. 3:10–11). He knew he had not yet achieved that goal, but he was determined to keep going. He said, "I press on to take hold of that for which Christ Jesus took hold of me" (v. 12). When I see or hear the word *press*, I often think of a bench press or a leg press. When a person is working out with weights, trying to press heavier ones, they sometimes come to a near stop and then really exert themselves. What they are doing at that moment is "pressing into" the weight in order to get it to move. In the same way people push themselves to new limits physically, Paul said he did so to become like Jesus. Instead of turning away from Jesus when life gets difficult, press more into him.

Paul switched analogies from a person lifting weights to a sprinter, looking straight ahead and pushing his chest forward to cross the finish line. He wrote, "But one thing I do: Forgetting what is behind and straining toward what is ahead, I press on toward the goal to win the prize for which God has called me heavenward in Christ Jesus" (vv. 13–14).

Are you determined to get in shape and exercise so you can enjoy a higher quality of life? Are you as determined to strive and become like Jesus? I desperately want to be like Christ, but I know his work in me is not done, so I press on and keep running. What about you?

DAILY HEALTH TIP

A good way to exercise regularly is to get into a routine so it becomes a part of your life. Exercise at the same time of the day. Work out a schedule for what you are going to do on Monday, Wednesday, and Friday, and another schedule for Tuesday, Thursday, and Saturday.

QUESTIONS FOR REFLECTION

1. Have you started an exercise program in the past only to stop after a few times? Why did you stop? What can you do differently this time to keep on keeping on?

2. Who can you make yourself accountable to for your exercise program?

PRAYER FOR TODAY

Father, thank you for creating the human body to move, walk, and run. Guide me to find the right accountability partner to help me in my journey to better health—both physically and spiritually. In Jesus' name I pray. Amen.

DAY 3

❈

HEBREWS 12:1–13

No pain, no gain!
A friend once severely twisted his ankle playing basketball. He didn't get it X-rayed right away, and he spent a couple of days limping around. Since he couldn't put all his weight on his ankle, he walked around on his tip-toes. When he finally went and had it X-rayed, his doctor put him on crutches for three weeks. The doctor's advice was that if he couldn't walk correctly ("heel toe, heel toe," he said), my friend should not walk at all. When recovering from an injury, "no pain, no gain" is bad advice, and it could make matters worse. However, when it comes to pushing yourself beyond what you thought were your limits, no pain, no gain can be good advice.

The writer of Hebrews encourages us to keep running because there are people who have gone on before us in the grandstands cheering us on, as if we were near the finish line of a marathon. The writer says we should be motivated by their faithful examples, and we should get rid of everything that slows us down so we can "run with perseverance the race marked out for us" (v. 1). Then the writer gives us the no-pain-no-gain principle by stating, "Endure hardship as discipline. . . . No discipline seems pleasant at the time, but painful. Later on, however, it produces a harvest of righteousness and peace for those who have been trained by it" (vv. 7, 11).

Physically, as you begin to exercise, you will go through a period of time where your body rebels. Every muscle will hurt; spasm may even occur. Every joint in your body will scream. But in the long run, your body will be stronger. So fight through the fatigue and soreness. The reward is better health.

Likewise, spiritually you may go through difficult times. You may find out the more committed to Christ you become, the more difficult life becomes. But hang in there; your spiritual muscles are being developed and you will be stronger than you ever thought possible.

DAILY HEALTH TIP

Look for opportunities to be more active during the course of your workday. Take the stairs instead of the elevator. Park in the back of the parking lot and walk. Go to the mall during your lunch break and walk. Stand up and stretch for a few minutes every hour. There are plenty of opportunities to be active during the day if you will take advantage of them.

QUESTIONS FOR REFLECTION

1. Who are some faithful believers you have known who have died and are now numbered with the "cloud of witnesses," cheering you on? Are you running a race for which they can be proud?

2. Can you think of a difficult time you went through spiritually that now, looking back, you know made you stronger? Can you think of a physical injury you had that took daring determination to overcome? How can you apply that same determination to your spiritual life?

PRAYER FOR TODAY

Lord God, thank you for all the examples you have given me of people who have run a good spiritual race. Thank you for the difficult times that have developed my spiritual strength. I pray you will take the physical pain I am experiencing right now and use it to make me stronger. Thank you for loving me and caring about every detail of my life. In the strong name of Jesus I pray. Amen.

DAY 4

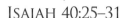

ISAIAH 40:25–31

People who often engage in running, swimming, biking, or other activities for long distances describe an interesting phenomenon known as the "second wind." After they exerted a certain amount of energy and effort, they would go through a time where continuing seemed nearly impossible, and they would begin to think they would not be able to finish. But then, as they fought that feeling and pressed, something amazing would happen: they would get their second wind and find the strength to complete the miles, laps, or whatever.

What is a second wind? It's not a scientific term, but a second wind occurs when you are exerting yourself mentally or physically. You reach a point of exhaustion, and everything within you is saying, "Stop! Quit! You can't go any further!" But as you refuse to quit, and keep pushing yourself, something unexpected occurs. Your body quits aching, you get more energy, and almost effortlessly (sometimes robotically), you keep going, no longer feeling the pain and fatigue.

When we become spiritually fatigued and are ready to quit, the prophet Isaiah tells us where our second wind originates.

In Isaiah 40, God comforted his people, letting them know that their time of trial was almost over. He encouraged them to trust in his sovereignty—"To whom will you compare me?" (v. 25)—and to rely on his strength. The prophet says, God "will not grow tired or weary, and his understanding no one can fathom" (v. 28).

It is precisely because of God's sovereignty, strength, and wisdom that he can be trusted, and when we trust him instead of ourselves, he gives us his strength. He gives us our second wind so we can continue (vv. 30–31). When we place our hope in him, he renews our strength, enabling us to soar like eagles and run and walk without getting tired (v. 31).

I love the picture the prophet paints of an eagle in flight. The eagle, with its beauty, majesty, grace, and power, harnessing the wind and soaring at great speed without flapping its wings, is something to behold. God is telling us to quit flapping our own wings, and to soar on the power he has provided.

DAILY HEALTH TIP

One way to stay consistent with your exercise program is to use variety. Variety is the spice of life and will keep things from getting monotonous. Swim one day, walk the next, jog the next, lift weights the next, go on a bike ride the next, and so on and so forth.

QUESTIONS FOR REFLECTION

1. In what ways can relying on God's wisdom and strength make your life easier?

2. What do you think it means to say that God will renew our strength and enable us to "soar on wings like eagles" (v. 31)?

PRAYER FOR TODAY

Father God, teach me to soar with you, relying on your wisdom and strength, instead of relying on my own resources. Forgive me for when I choose to do things my own way. As I press on, I trust in you to renew my strength and enable me to soar like an eagle. In the mighty name of Jesus I pray. Amen.

DAY 5

PROVERBS 4:18–27

R unning is one of the simplest yet most challenging forms of exercise. You can run nearly anywhere—on pavement, gravel, grass, or dirt. Or you can run in place or on a treadmill in the privacy of your own home. Running requires a minimum of equipment: comfortable clothes and a suitable pair of shoes. If you like running, more power to you. But running is also a demanding discipline—physically and mentally—and can result in unexpected aches and even injuries. When you run, you have to watch your steps carefully and make sure the path you are running is passable.

Many people who run or do other exercise outside prefer to do so in the morning before daylight so they can witness that "first gleam of dawn" (v. 18). There is something life affirming about the beginning of a new day. Each new day offers hope, and the writer of Proverbs said that is what the path of the righteous is like. Running at night can be tricky. There are things along the way that could make you stumble, things you will never see until it is too late; and that is what the "way of the wicked" is like (v. 19).

One great thing about running is that it gets your heartbeat going. Running is great cardiovascular exercise, and we all know the heart is the most important muscle. Likewise, spiritually, the greatest cardiovascular exercise we can do is to listen to the wisdom found in God's Word, apply it to our lives, and obey it. The writer of Proverbs tells us to keep words of wisdom within our hearts (v. 21), "for they are life to those who find them and health to a man's whole body" (v. 22). Physically and spiritually, there is nothing more important than taking care of your heart, "for it is the wellspring of life" (v. 23).

All week long, our focus has been on the importance of exercising to remain in good health. Along the way, an attempt has been made to point out a connection between physical exercise and spiritual growth. The better our health is, physically, the better we can serve God by serving others. Letting our physical health decline not only harms us physically, but it also takes its toll spiritually. The purpose for making this connection is to motivate us to see that physical exercise is a must so we can be all God wants us to be. Physical exercise is a necessity if we desire to live a life of total quality.

DAILY HEALTH TIP

Drink lots of water. Drink a cup of water before, during, and after your work out. Also, it is best not to exercise right after meals, or when it is extremely hot or humid.

QUESTIONS FOR REFLECTION

1. What do you think it means to describe the path of the righteous as "the first gleam of dawn" (v. 18)? How would you
   describe that analogy to someone else?

2. How would you explain the connection between physical exercise
   and spiritual growth? What does that connection mean to you?

PRAYER FOR TODAY

Lord, thank you for this week and the emphasis on exercise, both
physical and spiritual exercise. I trust your saving and sanctifying
work in my heart. Help me to take care of my physical body so that I
can be the best I can be for you. I pray in the name of your Son Jesus.
Amen.

RECOMMENDED READING

Total Quality Life, chapter 4, pages 58–59; chapter 8, pages 121–125

Imagine being part of a family whose members have been slaves— working continuously, without a day off, break, or vacation—for the last four hundred years. Imagine working all those years yourself without a break, and then, suddenly, you are set free. The only condition of your freedom is to leave the country where you've been enslaved and begin a long journey across a hot desert. Before, you lived in a state of bondage, but now, each day is a fight for survival. Each day, you journey in the hot sun and search for a single day's worth of food and water for you and your family. One day, a man stands before the entire clan, claiming he has heard from God. The man tells you, among other things, that God has said you are to rest on the last day of the week. You are not to work or even gather food and water.

Is he insane? You and your family are barely surviving on what you gather day-to-day. How can you take an entire day off to do nothing but rest?

Total quality life requires total quality health, and an important component of good health is getting adequate rest.

DAY 1

EXODUS 20:1–17

Many believers will tell you that in today's culture, keeping a weekly Sabbath is not practical, and since we are now under grace and not under the law, there is no reason to even try to keep the Sabbath. Even though we are under grace, we still need adequate rest.

The fourth commandment (vv. 8–11) is the longest commandment and includes the most explanation.

The word *Sabbath* means "to rest from labor." The basis for taking a weekly day to rest is the example of God during creation week, when God worked six days then rested on the seventh. The word *holy* means to "set apart as consecrated." The Sabbath command is to take one day in seven and separate that day to God by resting your body and renewing your soul. You were not made to keep going and going and going. Your body needs time to recover, and you need a reminder that all you have is from God. Your total dependence is on him. If the Israelites, who were in a life-and-death struggle for survival, could take a day off each week to rest, relax, reflect, and reenergize, then so can you. Your body needs it; your soul needs it; and God commands it.

DAILY HEALTH TIP

If you usually wake up tired, you may have some type of sleep disorder. Schedule an appointment with your doctor to discuss the possibility of a sleep study. Check with your insurance to see if it will pay for such a study.

QUESTIONS FOR REFLECTION

1. When was the last time you took a day off to relax and rejuvenate your body and soul? What excuses have you made for not taking a day off? When was the last time you went on a vacation?

2. For most Christians, Sunday has become the Sabbath. But Sundays have also become one of the busiest days of the week. What can you do this Sunday to truly rest and reflect on the goodness of God?

PRAYER FOR TODAY

Heavenly Father, help me to keep the principle of the Sabbath without becoming legalistic. Teach me to see that a day of rest is needed, not only for my body, but also for my soul. In Jesus' name I pray. Amen.

DAY 2

MARK 2:23–28

Part of yesterday's prayer was, "Help me to keep the principle of the Sabbath without becoming legalistic." This can be a difficult thing to do.

The original Sabbath commandment prohibited any type of physical labor. Later Jewish scholars defined and redefined the definition of physical labor. In other words, they forgot the principle of a day of rest and made it into a matter of keeping the law. Jesus violated their legalism. Here is what happened.

Jesus and his disciples, on a Sabbath day, were walking through a grain field (the walking violated the rule), and as they walked, they pulled the heads of grain off with their hands, rubbed their hands together to separate the husks from the kernels, blew the lighter husks away, and then ate the kernels. The Pharisees considered what they did physical labor, so they condemned them for violating the fourth commandment.

You might be thinking, wouldn't they also be guilty of stealing the grain? The answer is no. Under the Mosaic law, landowners were required to leave some grain for travelers to pick (see Deut. 23:25). What Jesus and his disciples did was permissible, but the Pharisees objected because they did it on the Sabbath. Separating the husks from the kernels was considered threshing, and blowing the husks away was considered winnowing. Both, according to the Pharisees' tradition, violated the Sabbath law.

Jesus reminded them that David had done something similar (see 1 Sam. 21:1–9), and then he identified the principle behind the law by saying, "The Sabbath was made for man, not man for the Sabbath" (Mark 2:27). In other words, God established the Sabbath principle of rest for the benefit of people, not to put them in bondage to rules and regulations. God did not need to take a day off at the end of creation week because he was tired. He took a day off to show us how important rest is to our overall health.

Did you know you can live longer without food and water than you can without sleep? That should tell us the importance of rest. There is nothing spiritual about working days and weeks without a break. In fact, doing so could be considered immoral. The Sabbath principle teaches us to trust God every day and follow his example because he knows what is best for us. Observing a day of rest and renewal reminds us of our total dependence on God.

DAILY HEALTH TIP

Most adults need between seven and nine hours of sleep every night to maintain optimum health. A lack of adequate sleep could lead to health problems like obesity, high blood pressure, diabetes, and premature aging. So, make sure you're getting enough sleep.

QUESTIONS FOR REFLECTION

1. How do you think you can keep the principle of a consistent Sabbath rest without becoming legalistic? Why should you even try?

2. How much sleep do you average each night? Is that enough? What can you do to get more rest?

3. Do you agree with the statement that working days and weeks without a break could be considered immoral? Why or why not?

PRAYER FOR TODAY

Creator God, thank you for caring so much for humanity that you built rest into our systems. Help me to achieve high-quality rest so I can be more productive for you and my family. I pray this in Jesus' name. Amen.

DAY 3

MATTHEW 11:25–30

Have you ever had the experience of trying to solve a problem, work with your hands, or finish a project, and you just can't seem to get it right? And the more you try, the more mistakes you make? The best thing you can do in that situation is to stop, rest, and get back to it later. It's amazing how things can look different and even easier after a good night's sleep.

When we push ourselves harder and become fatigued, small problems become big, and minor issues become major. Sometimes the best thing you can do physically, emotionally, and spiritually, is to take a nap. The importance of rest cannot be overstated. In today's Scripture reading, we learn where real rest comes from.

When my boys were babies, I loved to watch them sleep. A sleeping baby is the epitome of rest and peace. As an adult, don't you wish you could rest like a child? Jesus reminds us of the importance of childlike faith in coming to God (vv. 25–26). He also reminds us that the only way to know God is by knowing him (v. 27).

Then Jesus issued an incredible invitation. He said (and still says today), "Come to me, all you who are weary and burdened, and I will give you rest" (v. 28). To be weary means to be tired from hard work. To be burdened means to be loaded down with a heavy weight. Work can be tiresome and life can be burdensome. Do you ever feel overworked, overwhelmed, and overstressed?

What you need is rest, and that is what Jesus invites you to have. But it's not only physical rest he wants to give you, but spiritual rest as well.

Jesus says that in him "you will find rest for your souls" (v. 29). Nothing can refresh the mind, body, and spirit like rest. Jesus did not come to add to the pressures of life. He came to redeem us from the pressures of life and give us rest. The rest Jesus gives keeps us safe in the middle of storms, calm in the middle of difficulties, and at peace in the middle of chaos.

DAILY HEALTH TIP

One very important aspect of mental health is learning to do nothing, allowing the mind time to idle and recharge. Learning to be idle allows you to gather your thoughts, gain perspective, and relieve stress. The Bible says, "Be still, and know that I am God" (Ps. 46:10).

QUESTIONS FOR REFLECTION

1. How would you describe the rest and peace of a sleeping baby? Do you think that type of rest and peace is possible as an adult? Why or why not?

2. How would you describe the spiritual rest that we can have in Christ Jesus to someone else?

PRAYER FOR TODAY

Dear Jesus, I very much want the rest that you offer. Right now, I come to you in childlike faith. I place my complete trust in you. O Lord, I pray for rest so my strength can be renewed. Thank you for loving me and for giving me both physical and spiritual rest. In your holy name. Amen.

DAY 4

❧

PSALM 37:1–11

By commanding us to rest, God is not advocating laziness. Quite the contrary. We were created to work and be active. But God knows we are most productive when we are rested. Life is not a sprint, but a marathon. You have to rest; you have to take a break if you desire to run the marathon of life effectively and efficiently.

It is easy to be envious of other people's success. At times, that envy motivates us to work harder and longer hours. During those times, we might be tempted to skip breakfast or lunch or to work weekends. "It's only temporary," we tell ourselves. "I'm just trying to get ahead." We work hard to keep up with the Joneses, and we don't understand why the Joneses are so successful when they are not living a godly life, while we struggle trying to do what is right.

David, the composer of Psalm 37, tells us not to be envious of such people because one day they will wither and die (vv. 1–2). Instead, we should "trust in the LORD and do good" (v. 3). It is never wrong to do right, and it is never a waste of time to do good.

If you will trust in God and delight in him, "he will give you the desires of your heart" (v. 4). And, as if that promise isn't enough, God promises to "make your righteousness shine like the dawn, the justice of your cause like the noonday sun" (v. 6). One day, God will set the record straight. One day, God will make things right. Meanwhile, rest in God's wisdom and power. "Be still before the LORD and wait patiently for him" (v. 7). When the time is right, "the meek will inherit the land and enjoy great peace" (v. 11).

So, don't worry yourself sick, and don't get your life out of balance trying to keep up with other people. Live the life God gave you, enjoying his presence and committing your all to him. In the end, you will not be sorry. In the end, God will give you what you most desire because what you most desire will be what he wants for you.

What a wonderful promise!

DAILY HEALTH TIP

Learn to take a power nap. A power nap lasts no longer than ten to twenty minutes and has proven to increase alertness and productivity during the workday. Longer naps can cause sustained drowsiness, but a short power nap in the middle of your day can provide a fresh burst of new ideas and energy.

QUESTIONS FOR REFLECTION

1. Have you ever been envious of people who are not following Jesus? What was the reason for your envy? How did you deal with it? Why is it so emotionally, physically, and spiritually draining to be envious of others?

2. What do you think it means to say, "The meek will inherit the land and enjoy great peace" (v. 11)?

PRAYER FOR TODAY

Heavenly Father, thank you for your love. I consecrate my life and my plans to you. No longer will I strive to keep up with other people. With your help, I will strive only to live for you, knowing that you know what is best. In the mighty name of Jesus I pray. Amen.

DAY 5

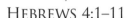

HEBREWS 4:1-11

This week we have been discussing the importance of adequate rest in maintaining optimal health. God has commanded that we rest. When we don't rest, we abuse our bodies and do harm to ourselves physically, emotionally, and spiritually. Today's passage teaches us that, ultimately, followers of Jesus Christ have been promised an eternal rest.

When I was learning to teach the Bible, I was taught that when you see the word *therefore* in the Bible, you should ask yourself, "What's the *therefore* there for?" The *therefore* of Hebrews 4:1 ties what the writer is about to say to what has been said in the previous chapter. Near the end of Hebrews 3, the writer discussed the Israelites and their failure to believe in the promise of God that they would enter the Promised Land, a land of rest. Now, today, God is still promising that we can enter his rest. Therefore, we should not be like the Israelites, who did not enter God's rest because of their unbelief. "For we also have had the gospel preached to us, just as they did; but the message they heard was of no value to them, because those who heard did not combine it with faith. Now we who have believed enter that rest" (vv. 2–3). Place your faith in Jesus Christ.

Are you entering the rest that God has promised? Are you tired of doing things your own way? Are you exhausted from carrying your own burdens? Are you fatigued by worrying about things you cannot control? Are you ready to take a break? Are you ready to rest?

In Jesus Christ, there is hope, peace, and rest. When you come to God and repent of your sins and place your faith in Jesus, you are promised eternal life. In addition, you are promised abundant life here on earth (see John 10:10).

"There remains, then, a Sabbath-rest for the people of God; for anyone who enters God's rest also rests from his own work, just as God did from his. Let us, therefore, make every effort to enter that rest" (Heb. 4:9–11).

DAILY HEALTH TIP

One of the single most important things you can do for your overall health and well-being is to learn to relax. When you relax, your body has an opportunity to unwind. Relaxing also slows your heart rate, reduces blood pressure, and increases blood flow to your muscles.

QUESTIONS FOR REFLECTION

1. What do you think it means to enter God's rest? Have you done so?

2. How can entering God's rest provide not only rest in eternity, but rest in this present life as well?

PRAYER FOR TODAY

Lord, sanctify my life by your love, mercy, and grace, so that I may enter into your rest. In the name of Jesus I pray. Amen.

REDUCE STRESS

RECOMMENDED READING

Total Quality Life, chapter 4, pages 61–62

Everyone has stress in their lives, but not all stress is bad. Feelings of stress are a natural reaction to the pressures and demands we face in life. Stress is one of our body's defense responses. Stress can serve to give us the extra energy and strength we need to accomplish a specific task. This type of positive stress, called eustress, is usually short-lived and can help you emotionally, mentally, and physically. However, most of the time when we talk about stress, we talk about the negative type of stress, known as distress. Distress can lead to anxiety, depression, ulcers, and a host of other physical problems. Distress can start immediately or can result from prolonged periods of eustress without allowing our bodies a chance to recover.

I am convinced most of the stress in our lives is self-imposed distress. We are overly stressed because of the lifestyles we have chosen to live. We are stressed because we have forgotten what is really important and because our lives are out of balance.

If you and I are going to live a healthy, total quality life, then we must learn how to deal with stress.

DAY 1

PSALM 27

M ark Twain once commented, "I have been through some terrible things in my life, some of which actually happened." Many people live in unfounded fear. Living that way can be extremely stressful. In Psalm 27, David put these unfounded fears into perspective. Since God is our light, our salvation, and our defender, we have nothing to fear and no reason to be afraid. Regardless of what we are facing— real or imagined—we can be confident that God is our protector, he hears our voice and will never leave or forsake us.

Whatever it is you are facing in life—whether pressures at home, work, church, or health—there is no need to be afraid. God may not immediately deliver you from your troubles, but he will walk with you through them. God is your stronghold, so "be strong and take heart and wait for the LORD" (v. 14).

DAILY HEALTH TIP

Stress—eustress or distress—can cause health problems or make health problems worse. If you feel some of your physical symptoms are caused by stress, make an appointment and talk about it with your doctor. It is important to make sure these symptoms are not caused by other health problems.

QUESTIONS FOR REFLECTION

1. How would you explain the difference between eustress and distress to someone else? Can you think of examples when you experienced good stress? Can you think of examples when you experienced bad stress?

2. What do you think it means to say God is your stronghold?

PRAYER FOR TODAY

Father God, life is so full of stress. At times, I feel pressure from so many different angles. Lord, I look to you for strength and help. I trust in you as my stronghold. I praise you for what you have done and what you will do. In Jesus' name I pray. Amen.

DAY 2

MATTHEW 6:25–34

Worry and stress often go together; worrying causes stress, and stress leads to worrying. People who worry a lot are usually less happy, and they tend to make those around them less happy too. In today's Scripture reading, Jesus speaks to our worry.

In the middle of Jesus' famous Sermon on the Mount, he said, "Therefore I tell you, do not worry" (v. 25). He told his disciples not to worry about their lives, bodies, clothes, food, or homes (vv. 25–31). He said that worrying about these things is what pagans do, not people who trust in God (v. 32). Jesus said, "Therefore do not worry about tomorrow, for tomorrow will worry about itself. Each day has enough trouble of its own" (v. 34).

Think of all the emotional energy we spend worrying about things we cannot control. Worrying about something does absolutely nothing to help or change the situation. After all, "Who of you by worrying can add a single hour to his life?" (v. 27).

Living a total quality life requires that we stop worrying and learn to trust God by seeking "first his kingdom and his righteousness" (v. 33). As we learn to do that, God promises he will take care of all the details about our lives that have caused us to worry.

DAILY HEALTH TIP

If you feel overwhelmed, prioritize. Do what you can do, and leave it all in God's hands. Address the problems you can solve, and don't worry about things you cannot control.

QUESTIONS FOR REFLECTION

1. Do you think worry is compatible with faith? Why or why not?

2. What do you think Jesus meant when he told us not to worry about tomorrow because "each day has enough trouble of its own" (v. 34)? Is this good news or bad news?

PRAYER FOR TODAY

Heavenly Father, I don't want my life to be wasted by fretting and worrying over things that are beyond my control. I give you all my worries and concerns, and I pray for your will to be done in my life. In the powerful name of Jesus I pray. Amen.

DAY 3

1 PETER 5:6–11

A n important first step in dealing with stress in your life is learning to recognize when you are feeling stressed. Some physical signs your body is under stress include tension in your shoulders and neck or clenching your hands into fists. When you sense your body responding to stress, it is time to take action to reduce that stress. Read the Bible, start praying daily, and seek to grow in God's grace. For some people, listening to Christian music helps reduce stress and release the tension in their muscles.

The apostle Peter wrote to give encouragement to a group of believers who were going through difficult times and tremendous stress. At the end of his beautiful letter, Peter told us the best way to deal with stress: "Cast all your anxiety on him because he cares for you" (v. 7). Let that promise sink in. To cast means to throw, and we are not told to throw some of our stress and anxiety on Jesus or just the really big stuff, but to throw all of our anxiety on him. Peter is using a play on words here. Other words for anxiety are *concern* or *worry*. Peter is saying, "Throw all your concerns on him because he is concerned for you." What a great promise!

What are you anxious about? What makes you concerned and worried? What keeps you up at night and causes that pain in your back or gives you a headache? The only solution is to take your anxiety and throw it to Jesus. Let your problems become his problems. He cares deeply for you and his shoulders are more than broad enough to carry you and what troubles you.

What happens when you transfer your anxiety to Jesus? The God who saved you by his grace and promises you eternal life will "restore you and make you strong, firm and steadfast. To him be the power for ever and ever. Amen" (vv. 10–11).

DAILY HEALTH TIP

Exercise is an excellent way to deal with stress. Exercise helps you relieve tension and releases chemicals into your brain that make you feel better. Exercise also helps you stay in shape and maintain better overall health.

QUESTIONS FOR REFLECTION

1. What are some physical signs that let you know when you are under a great deal of stress? What do you do when you first see those signs?

2. What are some things you can do as an outward expression of casting your anxieties on God? How would you explain what that means to someone else?

PRAYER FOR TODAY

Lord, through faith I am throwing all of my cares, concerns, and worries to you. I am asking you to relieve me of the stress I am under. Teach me how to deal with the stress in my life. Show me the changes I need to make and the things that I can do to reduce stress. Thank you for caring for me. In the majestic name of Jesus I pray. Amen.

DAY 4

PSALM 46

What do you fear? Whatever it is, there is probably a name for that fear. For example, do you fear failure? If so, you have a condition known as atychiphobia. Do you hate to read? If you do, you might have bibliophobia. Are you afraid of peanut butter getting stuck to the roof of your mouth? If so, then you suffer from arachibutyrophobia. And if you are afraid of fear itself, then you have phobophobia.

The psalmist says that even in the middle of your present trouble and even if the whole earth should collapse, there is still no reason to fear because God is "our refuge and strength" (v. 1).

Even in a time of war, natural disasters, and man-made calamities, God is still our fortress. He speaks and "the earth melts" (v. 6) and "wars cease to the ends of the earth" (v. 9). God is in control when things are going well, and he is in control when things are chaotic.

Instead of living in fear, our response should be to "be still, and know that [he is] God" (v. 10). The Hebrew word translated "be still" could also be translated "relax." There is no need to be afraid; there is no need to be stressed. Take a deep breath, relax, and then you will know that God is God, and he is still in control.

A friend who likes scuba diving once told me that if you get tangled in fishing line or some other obstruction while diving, your natural instinct is to try to fight your way out. But the more you try to fight the entanglement, the more entangled you become. The best thing to do is to relax, stop moving, and be still. Once you have done that, you can calmly get yourself out of the situation.

We live our lives at a hectic pace and rarely take time to relax. When faced with difficulties, we immediately try to fight our way out. But often, all the fighting makes the situation worse. We need to stop, be quiet, and wait until we hear from God. Then we can get ourselves out of the tangles and snares and move forward. When faced with difficulties, trials, and tribulations, we can either be stressed or get still.

DAILY HEALTH TIP

Train your body to relax. Start with one muscle. Hold it tight for a few seconds and then relax. Start with the muscles in your feet and work your way up through the rest of your body. Stretch and get going!

QUESTIONS FOR REFLECTION

1. What are your deepest fears? (If you say you have no fears, maybe you have a fear of being vulnerable. Everyone has fears.) What do you do to control those fears?

2. What can you do this week to relax and be still so you can hear from God? What changes do you need to make to your schedule to allow time to relax and be still?

PRAYER FOR TODAY

Father, thank you for being my refuge and strength. Thank you for always being in control, even when things seem out of control. I pray that you will teach me to relax and be still in the midst of difficulties so I can hear from you. In the peaceful name of Jesus I pray. Amen.

DAY 5

Jesus' disciples were getting a little stressed because they were not sure what was going to happen next. Jesus had been telling them he was leaving and that they were not to be troubled because he would return for them. But the disciples didn't feel ready for him to go. Jesus comforted them by telling them that when he left he would not leave them alone. Rather, he would send someone to comfort, teach, and walk with them—a Counselor.

The Greek word translated "Counselor" is *parakletos*, which means "one called alongside another." This Counselor is the Holy Spirit. As a follower of Jesus Christ, I have no reason to fear because the Holy Spirit, the third person of the Trinity, is always with me. The Holy Spirit is more than a conscience, or a still small voice telling me right from wrong. He is much better than a spirit guide or mantra. The Holy Spirit is God himself—a real person who wants a personal relationship with me.

Jesus described the Holy Spirit as "another Counselor" (v. 16). What he meant was that the Holy Spirit would be another of the same kind, not another of a different kind. In other words, Jesus was promising another Counselor, just like himself. The implication is that the Holy Spirit is to you and me what Jesus was to his disciples. What an awesome thought! Through the Holy Spirit, we have access to the same person, power, and potential the disciples had through Jesus Christ. The way the Holy Spirit will be to us what Jesus was to the disciples is by teaching us and reminding us of everything Jesus has taught (v. 26). "Peace

I leave with you; my peace I give you. . . . Do not let your hearts be troubled and do not be afraid" (v. 27).

We can be overwhelmed by stress when we try to do things and handle difficulties by ourselves. Jesus did not want us to live life that way. The Holy Spirit is there to walk beside us and to take the stress from our lives by guiding us and reminding us of the promises of God.

DAILY HEALTH TIP

Develop a hobby. Find something you enjoy doing that is totally unrelated to what you do for a living. Developing such a hobby will get your mind off your circumstances, challenge your mind, and prove to be a valuable source of stress relief.

QUESTIONS FOR REFLECTION

1. What do you think it means to say that the Holy Spirit has been called to come alongside you? Do you find that truth comforting? How, and in what way?

2. What do you think it means to say that the Holy Spirit is to you and me what Jesus was to the disciples? How would living out that truth reduce stress in your life?

PRAYER FOR TODAY

Dear Father, thank you for your Son who died for me, and thank you for your Holy Spirit who is with me now, walking alongside me, guiding me in your truth. Sanctify me by your Spirit to walk in your truth and rest in your power. In Jesus' name I pray. Amen.

AVOID HARMFUL SUBTANCES AND BEHAVIORS

RECOMMENDED READING
Total Quality Life, chapter 4, page 63; chapter 7, pages 111–113

Total quality health involves avoiding harmful substances and behaviors. Some harmful substances and behaviors are obvious—like illegal drugs or abuse of alcohol. Others are not as obvious—like nicotine, fatty foods, abuse of prescription drugs, and a host of other things. As we go through this week, every day's Scripture reading will come from the apostle Paul.

DAY 1

ROMANS 6:1–14

We are no longer under the law but grace, and I am so thankful for that fact. However, not being under the law is not a license to do whatever we feel like doing. Grace frees us, not so we can break the law, but so we can be free from the bondage of the law and sin to live a life that is holy and pleasing to God.

The purpose of the laws in the Old Testament was to show us how perfect and holy God is, how sinful we really are, and our need for a Savior. Before grace, we did not have the power to be free from sin. We were slaves to our natural desires. In our degenerate state, our bodies were instruments of wickedness (v. 13).

But now, because of the grace of God in Jesus Christ, we have died to sin and have been set free. Our bodies are no longer to be abused because now we belong to God as "instruments of righteousness" (v. 13). "For sin shall not be your master, because you are not under law, but under grace" (v. 14).

Do you see the application to your health and the importance of avoiding harmful substances? What you place in your body is a sign of whose instrument you are. Another word for *instrument* is *tool*. Your body is either a tool used for destruction or a tool in the hands of the Master Carpenter. Don't abuse God's instrument—your body—by feeding it unhealthy substances or by allowing it to rust, corrode, or breakdown for lack of care.

DAILY HEALTH TIP

I know it sounds cliché, but the first step to overcoming any type of addiction is admitting you have an addiction. Once you admit that some substance or activity has control of you, it is easier to get control back. Remember, however, as a follower of Jesus Christ, self-control is ultimately Holy Spirit control. Admit you have a problem and you need Holy Spirit power to conquer that problem.

QUESTIONS FOR REFLECTION

1. How do you think recognizing you are under grace and not under law should motivate you to live a holy life?

2. What steps can you take, this week, to ensure your body is used as a tool for righteousness and not a tool for wickedness?

PRAYER FOR TODAY

Dear God, teach me what it means to have died to sin and been brought back to life in Christ. Cleanse me and set me apart to live a Spirit-controlled life. Forgive me for how I have abused my body in the past. Today, I offer myself to you as an instrument of righteousness. In the strong name of Jesus. Amen.

DAY 2

ROMANS 6:15–23

Did you know there are more people in slavery today than at any other time in human history? Some human rights organizations estimate that as many as twenty million people worldwide are in bondage, and an alarming number of slaves are children. Spiritually speaking, you were born into slavery, but now, if you have placed your faith in Jesus Christ, you have been set free in order to be a slave to God.

In Paul's day, one in four persons was a slave, and many of those slaves had converted to Christianity. Consider the before and after picture Paul painted for them and us. Before you were saved by grace, you were a slave to sin, but now that you have been saved by grace, you are a slave to God, or at least that is what you are supposed to be. Being a slave to sin is described as a bondage that leads to death. Whereas being a slave to God is described as a blessing that leads to eternal life. The question is not, "Are you a slave?" The question is, "Whose slave are you?"

An addiction could be defined as the compulsive physiological or psychological need for a specific substance or activity to the point that it interferes with your relationships to other people, work, family, friends, and God. The addiction could be to something that is harmful or to something that is not necessarily harmful, but becomes harmful because of the unhealthy control it has on your life. A person who has become addicted to any substance or activity—whether cocaine, alcohol, prescription drugs, tobacco, caffeine, food, sex, or too much television—has become a slave to that substance or activity.

And here is Paul's point: You are a slave to God and therefore ought not to be a slave to anything else. Through grace, you have been set free from all addictions. Live in that freedom and become a slave to righteousness. "For the wages of sin is death, but the gift of God is eternal life in Christ Jesus our Lord" (v. 23).

DAILY HEALTH TIP

Joining a support group can be a healthy way to help overcome an addiction. Support groups let you know you are not alone and that you are not the only person struggling with your addiction. Support groups also make you accountable to other people. Find a Christ-centered, church-based support group and get involved. Trust Christ to transform your life.

QUESTIONS FOR REFLECTION

1. How would you describe the difference between being a slave to sin which leads to death and a slave to righteousness which leads to life? Whose slave are you?

2. How is an addict a slave to his or her addiction?

3. If a person has been set free through faith in Jesus Christ, why is it so easy to fall back into harmful addictions?

PRAYER FOR TODAY

Lord, my allegiance is to you. I pray that you would help me to overcome my dependence on anything other than your love and grace. Help me to rest contentedly in the good gifts that you provide. In the name of Jesus I pray. Amen.

DAY 3

1 CORINTHIANS 6:12–20

I f we are not careful, we have a tendency to swerve into one of two ditches in trying to live the Christian way. One ditch is legalism. The legalist values keeping a list of rules and regulations. It causes us to think we are more spiritual than others when we are faithful to our list of rules in ways others are not. The other ditch, and just as dangerous, is license. License is the attitude that it really doesn't matter how I live my life since I am saved by grace. As long as I believe in Jesus, how I live my life is of little consequence. How do we stay in the lane and not swerve into either ditch?

Since we are saved by grace and not by the law, there is a temptation to think "everything is permissible for me" (v. 12). Practically, however, "not everything is beneficial" (v. 12). There may not be a specific amount of time that means you've watched too much TV, but watching twenty hours every day is not beneficial for you spiritually, physically, relationally, or emotionally. Technically, you may be able to justify many things, but practically, it's better to have the attitude that "I will not be mastered by anything" (v. 12) other than the Holy Spirit.

Some of the habits you have may seem harmless, but do they add value to your life? Do they make you a better father, mother, husband, wife, son, or daughter? Do they help your spiritual growth? If not, consider eliminating them, not because you have to, but because you desire to live a better, more abundant, total quality life.

Our natural impulses are temporary; we were created for more than satisfying our natural desires (vv. 13–17). Sacrificing what we temporarily desire for the sake of God has eternal value. Paul's advice was that we stay as far away from immorality as we possibly can. For all those other things that are permissible but not beneficial, Paul exhorted that our bodies are the dwelling place of the Holy Spirit, "Therefore honor God with your body" (v. 20).

DAILY HEALTH TIP

If you have any kind of addiction, talk to a professional. This could be a counselor or a minister. Talking to someone will shed light on your thought process and the circumstances that may trigger your addictive behavior. When you talk to a professional, make sure they have a Christian worldview and that you are completely honest with him or her. Failing to do both could do more harm than good.

QUESTIONS FOR REFLECTION

1. What are some habits you have justified because they are not really wrong even though they are not beneficial? Are you willing to let go of that habit in order to grow closer to God? Why or why not?

2. How, and in what ways, can you begin to "honor God with your body" (v. 20)?

PRAYER FOR TODAY

Dear God, I ask that you show me those things in my life that may be permissible but are not beneficial. Grant me the strength to give up those temporary impulses for eternal values. I thank you for your Holy Spirit that dwells within me. In Jesus' name I pray. Amen.

DAY 4

❧

1 CORINTHIANS 8:1–13

The Christians living in Corinth could buy meat in the marketplace, where the meat was lower quality and higher priced, or at the local pagan temple, where the meat was higher quality and lower priced. The origin of the temple meat was well-known—it came from worshipers' offerings to a pagan god. The origin of the marketplace meat was often not known—it may have come from the temple or some other source.

As a result, Christians who consumed meat were faced with a dilemma: Should they shop for the best meat at a pagan temple or eat meat that could be associated with pagan worship? When they were guests in someone else's home and served meat that had been offered to idols, should they eat it?

Paul could have told the Corinthian believers to not worry about it and eat whatever they wanted whenever they wanted. But had he done this, he would have steered them into the ditch of license. Or, Paul could have advised them to avoid eating the meat under any condition. But had he done that, he would be steering them into the ditch of legalism.

Instead, Paul's advice to the Corinthian believers, as well as to us when we face those gray areas of not so right and not so wrong, was to exercise liberty with responsibility.

As a mature Christian, you may have discovered freedom, but you also have the responsibility to curb your liberty if it is going to harm a younger or more immature believer. Paul wrote, "Be careful, however, that the exercise of your freedom does not become a stumbling block to the weak" (v. 9). Furthermore, you should be willing to forsake, or cease to participate in that activity, even though you know it is not wrong, for the sake of the other, weaker person (v. 13).

When the Bible is clear, stand firm and don't compromise. But when the Bible is silent and there are differences of opinion among believers, be willing to curb your liberty for the sake of unity and maturity.

DAILY HEALTH TIP

Replace the time you might have spent participating in a questionable activity by volunteering that time to serve others. If you know that on a certain night of the week you will be tempted to do something you've chosen not to do, find a ministry organization that you can serve during that time instead.

QUESTIONS FOR REFLECTION

1. What are some issues believers face today about right and wrong that is similar to the issue in Paul's day about meat offered to idols? How do you usually handle a situation where believers see an issue or activity differently?

2. Why do you think Paul admonished those more mature in faith to compromise or refrain from certain activities for the sake of those weaker in faith?

PRAYER FOR TODAY

Lord, thank you for the simplicity and practicality of your Word. I pray you will help me see where I should give up my liberty for the sake of unity and maturity. God, help me to have the desire to give up things that are not wrong for the sake of you and others. In the wonderful name of Jesus I pray. Amen.

DAY 5

EPHESIANS 5:3–20

Paul made a list of things that should be avoided by a disciple of Jesus Christ. Some of the things are obvious, like sexual immorality and greed, but others are not so obvious, like "obscenity, foolish talk or coarse joking" (v. 4). When it comes to harmful substances, we usually think of things we put into our bodies, but here Paul mentions harmful substances that come out of our bodies through our speech. What goes in usually does come out. Jesus put it this way: "What goes into a man's mouth does not make him 'unclean,' but what comes out his mouth, that is what makes him 'unclean'" (Matt. 15:11).

Paul said that while you once were unclean, you are no longer to be that way because you have been brought from darkness to light (Eph. 5:8–11). "Live as children of light" (v. 8) and have nothing to do "with the fruitless deeds of darkness" (v. 11). As we have looked at the writings of Paul this week, a common theme has been that, though we were once unclean, we have been set free, so we ought to live like we have been set free.

This section closes with an admonition to be careful how we live because we represent Jesus Christ. As such, we shouldn't "get drunk on wine, which leads to debauchery. Instead be filled with the Spirit" (v. 18). Drunkenness is but one example. Whatever our addiction, we are to get rid of it and give ourselves instead to the control of the Holy Spirit. Lift other people up, encourage them in their journey of faith and "always [give] thanks to God the Father for everything, in the name of our Lord Jesus Christ" (v. 20).

DAILY HEALTH TIP

One of the most powerful weapons you have to fight addiction and return to a life of quality health is prayer. Prayer reminds you who is really in control, and it is through prayer you receive power to overcome. As you seek to be free of harmful substances and behaviors, don't forget to pray.

QUESTIONS FOR REFLECTION

1. What is the one thing you remember the most about your study this week? Why do you think that is the one thing that stands out?

2. What do you think is the relationship between the harmful substances people put in their bodies and the harmful statements that come out of their mouths?

3. What steps can you take today to surrender control of your life to the Holy Spirit?

PRAYER FOR TODAY

Lord, thank you for your convicting power and forgiving spirit. Thank you for the hope I have in Jesus and the help I have from the Holy Spirit. In Jesus' name I pray. Amen.

RECOMMENDED READING

Total Quality Life, chapter 4, page 63; chapter 8, pages 125–128

It's not fun getting older, but as you age, there are common-sense things you can do to gain and maintain total quality health. You know what those things are—exercise more, eat less, drink water, and get adequate rest. The only thing standing between you and better health is your determination and resolve to make changes in your life. However, some health problems are more significant and require professional medical treatment and oversight.

Many people hate going to the doctor. I am now at the age where I have to see my doctor at least once a year. Going to the doctor is not my favorite thing to do, but I am convinced that one of the best things a person can do to achieve total quality health is building a good relationship with their primary care doctor and visiting that doctor for check-ups on a regular basis.

Maintaining quality health by having regular check-ups is the topic for this week. These Bible studies will keep the topic of sickness, doctors, and healings in our minds, and the daily health tips will center on how to choose a primary care physician.

DAY 1

LUKE 1:1–4; ACTS 1:1–5; COLOSSIANS 4:14

I have always found it interesting that God chose a medical doctor to write two of the books in the New Testament. Luke, a physician, wrote the books of Luke and Acts in the Bible. A good medical doctor pays attention to details, and Luke made it clear at the beginning of both Luke and Acts that he was going to pay attention to details. But what else do we know about Dr. Luke?

More than likely, Luke was from Antioch. Not much is known about his life, and he is only referred to by name three times in the New Testament. It is obvious from his writings that he knew Theophilus, a wealthy government official. A common practice in that day was for wealthy slave owners to educate capable slaves as physicians and then grant them their freedom. There is some evidence that Luke was a common slave name, and some scholars have speculated that Luke was born as a slave in Theophilus's household, trained as a physician, and then granted freedom.

From the New Testament, we know that Luke traveled with Paul on some of his missionary journeys and was with Paul during his imprisonment in Caesarea. Luke was obviously a man of integrity and humility. His writings make up over one-fourth of the New Testament, but he never mentioned himself by name. His writings, especially his gospel, show that he was passionate about helping the poor, sick, and outcast. Luke truly had a physician's heart.

If you do not have a primary care physician, you need to find one. As you look for a doctor, look for someone who has the same characteristics as Dr. Luke. He was a man of faith, loyalty, humility, integrity, and compassion; he paid attention to details.

DAILY HEALTH TIP

When choosing a primary care doctor, the most important thing you can do is your homework. Make sure to get referrals from your family and friends, check the doctor's credentials and insurance coverage, and most importantly, ask lots of questions.

QUESTIONS FOR REFLECTION

1. What do you think are the most important characteristics of a doctor?

2. Why do you think some people hate going to the doctor? When was the last time you went to the doctor?

PRAYER FOR TODAY

Lord, thank you for choosing a man like Luke to write parts of the New Testament and for his example of faith, loyalty, integrity, and humility. Thank you, Father, for giving men and women today the capability of learning and practicing medicine. Please guide me in my choice of physicians and guide them in providing care for me. In Jesus' name I pray. Amen.

DAY 2

MATTHEW 9:9–13

In ancient Rome, individuals could purchase the rights to collect taxes
from territories that had been conquered. Of the taxes collected, they
would owe a certain amount to Rome, then pocket the rest. So, a tax
collector could make as much money as he could extract from the
people, completely protected by the government. In order to get such a
job, Matthew must have already been a wealthy businessman; and the
only reason to become a tax collector was to become even wealthier.

To a Jewish person in the first century, the only thing worse than
a tax collector would have been a Jewish tax collector. They were
considered traitors. The Jewish Talmud (an ancient commentary on
the Old Testament) taught that it was righteous to lie and deceive a
tax collector because it was what a professional extortionist
deserved. Tax collectors were the lowest of the low. After Jesus
reached out to Matthew, the tax collector invited Jesus to his house
for dinner. Matthew's house was probably large enough to host a
hundred or more guests, so this banquet probably included dozens
more "tax collectors and 'sinners'" (v. 10) as guests. Jesus was
keeping bad company, and the Pharisees later told him so. Jesus
responded to the Pharisees, "It is not the healthy who need a doctor,
but the sick. . . . For I have not come to call the righteous, but sinners"
(vv. 12–13).

Jesus is the Great Physician. As his followers, we have the
prescription that cures the loneliness, depression, and anxiety of lost
people. We have the hope that the world needs. It is not the people

who consider themselves healthy who will benefit from this cure; rather, it is those who recognize themselves as spiritually sick who can gain from the hope Jesus offers. It is time for all of us to become medical missionaries, reaching out to the sick and offering the mercy and grace of God.

DAILY HEALTH TIP

Once you have done your homework and chosen a doctor, schedule an appointment to get a complete physical examination. At the end of the examination, ask your doctor, "What do I need to do to improve my health?" Then, make a commitment to follow your doctor's advice.

QUESTIONS FOR REFLECTION

1. What do you think Jesus meant when he said, "It is not the healthy who need a doctor, but the sick" (v. 12)? How would you explain what he meant to someone else?

2. What implications does Jesus' statement have on how and to whom you reach out with the hope of Christ?

PRAYER FOR TODAY

Heavenly Father, I was spiritually sick and you healed me. What you did for me you can do for others. Help me to reach out to the sick, poor, and those who have no hope. Break my heart and fill me with compassion for the lost. In Jesus' name I pray. Amen.

DAY 3

JAMES 5:13–20

Occasionally, medical journals will publish articles about the effects of prayer on the healing process. Some studies seem to show that patients who pray have a quicker recovery from sickness and surgery. Often, the explanation given for the data is that people who pray and have others praying for them experience a greater sense of hope and support from their family and friends. The conclusions drawn typically leave little space for believing that prayer works because God answers prayer.

The word *trouble* in today's reading (v. 13) refers to hardship or distress. When such hardships come, our first response should be to pray. If, on the other hand, you are not suffering at the moment, you should "sing songs of praise" (v. 13). Every day—at every moment— you have a reason to either pray or praise.

James admonishes that if anyone is sick, they "should call the elders of the church to pray over him and anoint him with oil in the name of the Lord" (v. 14). Some of the most precious times I have had with my church family have been gathered around someone who is sick, praying for them, laying hands on them, and anointing them with oil. Miraculous healings can occur through such times. And even when God chooses not to heal, congregations grow closer through laying someone's sickness at God's feet. This is another kind of miracle.

Perhaps you know someone like the young mother who was told she had cancer. Her church fasted and prayed with her. And when she had her follow-up exam to determine the severity of the cancer, it was gone without a trace! While such dramatic results may not be everyday occurrences, God does still heal and forgive when we pray. "The prayer of a righteous man is powerful and effective" (v. 16). Go to your doctor; follow his or her advice; take your medicine; have that surgery. But through it all, don't forget to pray.

DAILY HEALTH TIP

The best time to choose a doctor is now, before you need one. When you are sick or in the middle of an emergency, you will not have the time to check referrals and do your homework. If you do not already have a doctor, begin the process of choosing one today. You will not be sorry.

QUESTIONS FOR REFLECTION

1. Do you believe God still heals? Why or why not? Do you know someone who experienced a miraculous healing?

2. Why do you think prayer works in helping people who are sick or recovering from a sickness? Do you believe in the power of prayer? Why or why not?

PRAYER FOR TODAY

Dear Jesus, you are the Great Physician, and I thank you for the privilege to bring my needs and concerns for friends, family, and myself to you. I trust in you to provide whatever kind of healing is most needed in the lives of those I love. I believe the prayer of faith makes me whole. In your almighty name I pray. Amen.

DAY 4

MARK 1:29–45

The Gospels were not intended to be a detailed (or even a chronological) biography of Jesus' life. The Gospels focus primarily on a three-year period of time, and the most space is dedicated to the last week of Jesus' life. But the glimpse these books give us of Jesus' ministry is meant to be a summary of the kinds of things he did and taught as he was inaugurating his kingdom, and the story we have is more than adequate. In fact, John said it would be impossible to write down everything that Jesus did (see John 20:30–31).

The day Mark described in today's passage started with Jesus traveling to Capernaum on the Sabbath and delivering a man from demon possession (see Mark 1:21–28). After leaving the synagogue, Jesus went to Peter's home and healed Peter's mother-in-law from a fever (vv. 29–31). That evening, "the whole town gathered at the door, and Jesus healed many who had various diseases" (vv. 33–34). Mark 1 ends with Jesus healing a man of leprosy (vv. 40–45).

Jesus said he "came to seek and to save what was lost" (Luke 19:10). The word *save* means "to be made whole again." So, Jesus came to make people whole—not only spiritually whole, but emotionally and physically whole as well. When Jesus heals a person, he makes that person whole and gives a glimpse into what life in his kingdom will be like. Our ultimate healing will come in the next life when we will live forever. But I am so thankful that, in this life, Jesus gives us a glimpse into heaven by healing us and making us whole again.

DAILY HEALTH TIP

In choosing a doctor, consider personal factors. Are you looking for a male or female doctor? It is vital that you feel comfortable with your doctor. You want a doctor who is kind, compassionate, and who will patiently listen to all your concerns and questions. Finally, take time to learn about the doctor's support staff. Chances are, when you call the office, those are the people who will answer your call.

QUESTIONS FOR REFLECTION

1. Have you ever imagined what it would have been like to have been an eyewitness to Jesus' life and ministry? If so, what are some of the things you imagined?

2. In what ways does being saved by Jesus mean to be made whole again? What areas of your life has Jesus made whole? What areas of your life need to be made whole?

PRAYER FOR TODAY

Dear God, I claim your sanctifying power to make me whole. Use me to bring your healing into someone else's life this week. In Jesus' name I pray these things. Amen.

DAY 5

❦

REVELATION 21:1–27

O ur bodies are God's temple, so we need to do all we can to live a healthy life. In order to maintain total quality health, we need to eat right, exercise regularly, get adequate rest, reduce our stress levels, avoid harmful substances, and have regular check-ups. Ultimately, our bodies will deteriorate. However, by staying in the best shape possible, we make our lives more comfortable, enjoyable, and productive. The good news is that in the next life, for all eternity, we will be in perfect health.

In today's passage, John describes what the new heaven and new earth will look like. Actually, John only describes one city, the New Jerusalem. It's a beautiful picture. Our eternal home is far greater, far more magnificent than mere words can describe. Read the chapter slowly, multiple times. Try to picture what John is describing.

While all of Revelation 21 is important and beautiful, I want to focus on verse 4: "He will wipe every tear from their eyes. There will be no more death or mourning or crying or pain, for the old order of things has passed away."

Imagine that! In heaven, there will be no more death, mourning, or crying. I think it is safe to assume that among other things this means that in heaven there will be no more sickness, cancer, heart attacks, diabetes, obesity, colds, allergies, or headaches—no more sickness of any kind.

Why will these things be absent? Because on the new earth, "no longer will there be any curse" (22:3). Because of sin, this entire universe has been cursed (see Gen. 3). Once Jesus returns, the curse will be destroyed, along with sickness and death.

"Behold, I am coming soon! Blessed is he who keeps the words of the prophecy in this book" (Rev. 22:7).

"Amen. Come, Lord Jesus" (22:20).

DAILY HEALTH TIP

In choosing a doctor, make sure the doctor practices relatively close to where you live and that he or she has admitting privileges at your preferred hospital. You do not want to drive long distances for an appointment, and if you ever do need to be hospitalized, you need to be able to go to the hospital of your choice.

QUESTIONS FOR REFLECTION

1. If in the end everyone dies, even those who have been healed, why does it matter so much that we take care of our bodies?

2. What sickness are you or someone close to you dealing with today? What does it mean to you to know that in the next life there will be no sickness? How does believing that truth help you deal with your present circumstance?

PRAYER FOR TODAY

Heavenly Father, I am overwhelmed by your love for me and by your promise that I will spend eternity with you in a place that is beyond description. Set me apart to love and serve you all the days of my life. Preserve me in good health so that I can bring honor and glory to you. In the name of Jesus I pray. Amen.

A Highland Regiment

LONDON : JOHN LANE, THE BODLEY HEAD
NEW YORK : JOHN LANE COMPANY MCMXVIII

Third Edition

*Printed in Great Britain
by Turnbull & Spears, Edinburgh*

To

THE OFFICERS AND MEN

OF THE 5TH SEAFORTH HIGHLANDERS

AND ESPECIALLY TO

MAJOR A. L MACMILLAN

WHO IS AND WILL BE

TO ME AS TO ALL THE REST

THE MAJOR FOR EVER

CONTENTS

I

8

A HIGHLAND REGIMENT

TO A PRIVATE SOLDIER

THE air is still, the light winds blow
  Too quietly to wake you now.
Dreamer, you dream too well to know
Whose hand set death upon your brow.
The shrinking flesh the bullets tore
Will never pulse with fear again ;
Sleep on, remembering no more
Your sudden agony of pain.

Oh, poor brave smiling face made naught,
Turned back to dust from whence you came,
You have forgot the men you fought,
The wounds that burnt you like a flame ;
With stiff hand crumbling a clod,
And blind eyes staring at the sky,
The awful evidence of God
Against the men who made you die.

You have forgotten, sleeping well,
But what of them ? shall they forget
Your body broken with the shell,
Your brow whereon their seal is set ?
Does earth for them hold any place
Where they shall never see the flies
Clustered about your empty face
And on your blind, accusing eyes ?

Good-night, good sleep to you.   But they
Will never know good-night again,
Whose eyes are seeing night and day,
The humble men who died in vain.
Their ears are filled with bitter cries,
Their nostrils with the powder smell,
And shall see your mournful eyes
Across the reeking fires of hell.

ANNS AN GLEANN'SAN ROBH MI OG

IN the Glen where I was young
    Blue-bell stems stood close together,
In the evenings dew-drops hung
Clear as glass above the heather.
I'd be sitting on a stone,
Legs above the water swung,
I a laddie all alone,
In the glen where I was young.

Well, the glen is empty now,
And far am I from them that love me,
Water to my knees below,
Shrapnel in the clouds above me;
Watching till I sometimes see,
Instead of death and fighting men,

Hold me close until I die,
Lift me up, it's better so ;
If, before I go, I cry,
It isn't I'm afraid to go ;
Only sorry for the boy
Sitting there with legs aswung
In my little glen of joy,
In the glen where I was young.

AUGUST, 1914

FROM A WAR STATION

To A. K. F.

IN Oxford now the lamps are lit,
   The city bells ring low,
And up and down the silent town
   The ghosts of friendship go.

With whispering laughs they meet and pass
   As we were used to do,
And somewhere in the airy crowd
   My spirit walks with you.

The troopers quarter in the rooms
   That once were yours and mine,
And you are lying out to-night
   Behind the firing-line.

But still in rooms that were our own
   We wander, you and I,
And night and day our spirits walk
   Along the empty High.

GOLSPIE, 1915

CHA TILL MACCRUIMEIN

DEPARTURE OF THE 4TH CAMERONS

THE pipes in the street were playing bravely,
  The marching lads went by,
With merry hearts and voices singing
  My friends marched out to die;
But I was hearing a lonely pibroch
  Out of an older war,
" Farewell, farewell, farewell, MacCrimmon,
  MacCrimmon comes no more."

And every lad in his heart was dreaming
  Of honour and wealth to come,
And honour and noble pride were calling
  To the tune of the pipes and drum;
But I was hearing a woman singing
  On dark Dunvegan shore,
" In battle or peace, with wealth or honour,
  MacCrimmon comes no more."

PUBLISHER'S NOTE.

We regret to say that since the second edition of this volume was published the author has been killed in action.

It is hoped to issue shortly a posthumous volume of his poems and prose pieces, which will bear the title of " WAR THE LIBERATOR," and will contain a Memoir and a Portrait.

And there in front of the men were marching,
   With feet that made no mark,
The grey old ghosts of the ancient fighters
   Come back again from the dark ;
And in front of them all MacCrimmon piping
   A weary tune and sore,
" On the gathering day, for ever and ever,
   MacCrimmon comes no more."

BEDFORD, 1915

TO A DEAD SOLDIER

SO I shall never see you more.
　　The northern winds will blow in vain
Brave and heart-easing off the shore.
You will not sail with them again.
I shall not see you wait for me
Where on the beach the dulse is brown,
Nor hear at night across the sea
Your chorus of the Nighean doun.

Are you so easy handled now
That Flanders soil can keep you still
Although the northern breezes blow
All day across the fairy's hill?
And can an alien lowland clay
Hold fast your soul and body too,
Or will you rise and come away
To where our friendship waits for you?

You cannot rest so far from home,
Your heart will miss the northern wind,
Back from the lowland fields will come,
Your soul the grave can never bind.
Once more your hands will trim the sail
That carries us across the bay
To where the summer islands pale
Over the seas and far away.

And you will sail and watch with me
The things we saw and loved before,
The happy islands of the sea,
The breakers white against the shore.
A hundred joys that we held dear
Will call you from the Flanders town,
And in the evenings I shall hear
Your chorus of the Nighean doun.

BEDFORD, 1915

THE WAITING WIFE

OUT on the hillside the wild birds crying,
  A little low wind and the white clouds flying,
A little low wind from the southward blowing,
What should I know of its coming and going ?

Over the battle the shrapnel crying
A tune of lament for the dead and the dying,
And a little low wind that is moaning and weeping
For the mouths that are cold and the brave hearts sleeping.

I and my man were happy together
In the summer days and the warm June weather—
What is the end of our laughter and singing ?
A little low wind from the southward winging.

The hearth is cold and my house is lonely,
And nothing for me but waiting only,
Feet round the house that come into it never,
And a voice in the wind that is silent for ever.

GOLSPIE, 1915

20

CHRIST IN FLANDERS

OH, you that took our sin and pain
  Upon your shoulders long ago,
Are you come back to earth again,
About the battle do you go ?
By trenches where with bitter cries
Men's spirits leave their tortured clay,
Oh, wanderer with the mournful eyes,
Are you on Flanders soil to-day ?

The battle fog is wreathed and curled
Before us, that we cannot see
The darkness of the newer world
As your eternal agony,
The gallant hearts, the bitter blood,
The pains of them that have not died,
A bright light in the eyes of God
And a sharp spear-point in his side.

Church Parade, 1915

HARVEST

ALONG the dusty highway,
  And through the little town,
The people of the country
Are riding up and down.
Behind the lines of fighting
They gather in all day
The harvest, folk are reaping
At home and far away.

If on the hills about us,
Where now the thrush sings low,
The face of earth were bitter,
It would not hurt us so.
Though earth grew strange and savage
And all the world were new,
It would not tear our memory
The way the cornfields do.

Oh, you that fought your battles
Beneath the Southern Cross,
The earth was kinder to you,
You could not feel your loss,
Nor waken every morning
And clear before you see
The grassy fields and meadows
Where you would wish to be.

But in a haunted corn-land
We move, as in a dream
Of quiet hills and hedges
And a swift-flowing stream,
And on the hills about us
Through all the din of war,
The home that we were born in,
And we shall see no more.

BUIRE-SUR-ANCRE, 1915

OXFORD FROM THE TRENCHES

THE clouds are in the sky, and a light rain falling,
   And through the sodden trench splashed figures come
   and go,
But deep in my heart are the old years calling,
And memory is on me of the things I used to know.

Memory is on me of the warm dim chambers,
And the laughter of my friends in the huge high-ceilinged hall,
Lectures and the voices of the dons deep-droning,
The things that were so common once—O God, I feel them all.

Here there are the great things, life and death and danger,
All I ever dreamed of in the days that used to be,
Comrades and good-fellowship, the soul of an army,
But, oh, it is the little things that take the heart of me.

For all we knew of old, for little things and lovely,
We bow us to a greater life beyond our hope or fear,
To bear its heavy burdens, endure its toils unheeding,
Because of all the little things so distant and so dear.

BÉCOURT, 1915

MISERERE

GONE is now the boast of power,
　　Strength to strike our foes again,
God of battles in this hour
Give us strength to suffer pain.
Lest the spirit's chains be rent,
Lest the coward flesh go free
Unto thee our prayer is sent,
　　Miserere Domine.

Death unseen beneath our feet,
Death above us in the sky,
Now before Thy judgment-seat
Grant us honourably to die.
Lustful, sinful, careless all,
In the martyr's road are we.
Lest from that high path we fall,
　　Miserere Domine.

Men that mocked Thee to Thy face,
Fools who took Thy name in vain—
Grant that in this deadly place
Jests and blasphemy remain.
On the pallid face of death,
Gasping slow and painfully
Curses with its latest breath,
    Miserere Domine.

Where we see the men we know
Rags of broken flesh and bone,
And the thing that hurt them so
Seems to wait for us alone,
Where the silence of the grave
Broods and threatens soundlessly,
On the souls we cannot save,
    Miserere Domine.

LA BOISSELLE, 1915

THE UNDYING RACE

HERE in the narrow broken way
  Where silently we go,
Steadfast above their valiant clay
  Forgotten crosses show.
Our whispers call to many a ghost
  Across the flare-light pale,
And from their graves the Breton host
  Stand up beside the Gael.

Year upon year of ancient sleep
  Have rusted on our swords,
But once again our place we keep
  Against the Saxon hordes.
Since Arthur ruled in Brittany,
  And all the world was new,
The fires that burned our history,
  Burn in our spirits too.

One speech beyond their memory
    Binds us together still,
One dream of home wherein we see
    River and sea and hill.
When in the night-time Fingal's peers
    Fight their old wars again,
The blood of twice two thousand years
    Leaps high in every vein.

Old songs that waked King Arthur's knights
    Stir in our memory yet,
Old tales of olden heroes fights
    That we cannot forget,
To die as Fingal's warriors died
    The great men long ago,
Breton and Gael stand side by side
    Against the ancient foe.

La Boisselle, 1915

28

IN NO MAN'S LAND

THE hedge on the left, and the trench on the right,
   And the whispering, rustling wood between,
And who knows where in the wood to-night
Death or capture may lurk unseen,
The open field and the figures lying
Under the shade of the apple trees—
Is it the wind in the branches sighing,
Or a German trying to stop a sneeze ?

Louder the voices of night come thronging,
But over them all the sound is clear,
Taking me back to the place of my longing
And the cultured sneezes I used to hear,
Lecture-time and my tutor's " handker "
Stopping his period's rounded close,
Like the frozen hand of the German ranker
Down in a ditch with a cold in his nose.

I'm cold, too, and a stealthy snuffle

From the man with a pistol covering me,

And the Bosche moving off with a snap and a shuffle

Break the windows of memory—

I can't make sure till the moon gets lighter—

Anyway shooting is over bold.

Oh, damn you, get back to your trench, you blighter,

I really can't shoot a man with a cold.

HAMMERHEAD WOOD
THIEPVAL, 1915

SNOW IN FRANCE

THE tattered grass of No Man's Land
    Is white with snow to-day,
And up and down the deadly slopes
    The ghosts of childhood play.

The sentries, peering from the line,
    See in the tumbled snow
Light forms that were their little selves
    A score of years ago.

We look and see the crumpled drifts
    Piled in a little glen,
And you are back in Saxony
    And children once again.

From joyous hand to laughing face
    We watch the snow-balls fly,
The way they used ere we were men
    Waiting our turn to die.

But for a little space of peace
   We watch them come and go,
The children that were you and I
   At play among the snow.

Bois d'Authuille, 1915

WHERE the light wraith of death goes dancing
　　In and out of the wavering line,
Now retreating and now advancing
Till opposite you he makes the sign,
Though the wind of his breath be on you,
Though in your flesh you feel the smart,
There have been worse things laid upon you,
Be steadfast and endure my heart.

There is no need of honour for you,
There is no gift the gods can send,
Only the weary days before you,
Only endurance to the end.
This remains that in all temptation
Still your head shall be lifted high.
You that have known a worse damnation,
Why should you be afraid to die ?

You that are dead and damned already,
How should you be afraid of death?
Strength remains to you firm and steady
Enduring still to your latest breath,
Eyes to see and ears for hearing,
Things and words you would fain forget,
And anger to slay the snake of fearing
That lives in the heart of the dead man yet.

Fear? If hope is a thing forgotten,
What can you fear the gods will do?
If the heart and kernel of life is rotten
What is the husk to trouble you?
Stand up straight to your work, be strong, lad,
Never a fear of bullet or shell,
You that have lived in hell for long, lad,
Needn't be fearing to die in hell.

THIEPVAL, 1915

34

MATRI ALMAE

CITY of hopes and golden dreaming
    Set with a crown of tall grey towers,
City of mist that round you streaming
    Screens the vision of vanished hours,
All the wisdom of youth far-seeing,
    All the things that we meant to do,
Dreams that will never be clothed in being,
    Mother, your sons have left with you.

Clad in beauty of dreams begotten
    Strange old city for ever young,
Keep the visions that we've forgotten,
    Keep the songs we have never sung.
So shall we hear your music calling,
    So from a land where songs are few
When the shadows of life are falling,
    Mother, your sons come back to you.

So with the bullets above us flying,
   So in the midst of horror and pain
We shall come back from the sorrow of dying
   To wander your magical ways again.
For that you keep and grow not older
   All the beauty we ever knew,
As the fingers of death grow colder,
   Mother, your sons come back to you.

In the Leave Train, 1915

BEFORE THE SUMMER

WHEN our men are marching lightly up and down,
   When the pipes are playing through the little town,
I see a thin line swaying through wind and mud and rain
And the broken regiments come back to rest again.

Now the pipes are playing, now the drums are beat,
Now the strong battalions are marching up the street,
But the pipes will not be playing and the bayonets will not
      shine,
When the regiments I dream of come stumbling down the line.

Between the battered trenches their silent dead will lie
Quiet with grave eyes staring at the summer sky.
There is a mist upon them so that I cannot see
The faces of my friends that walk the little town with me.

Lest we see a worse thing than it is to die,
Live ourselves and see our friends cold beneath the sky,
God grant we too be lying there in wind and mud and rain
Before the broken regiments come stumbling back again.

   CORBIE, 1916

TO MY SISTER

IF I die to-morrow
 I shall go happily.
With the flush of battle on my face
I shall walk with an eager pace
The road I cannot see.

My life burnt fiercely always,
And fiercely will go out
With glad wild fighting ringed around,
But you will be above the ground
And darkness all about.

You will not hear the shouting,
You will not see the pride,
Only with tortured memory
Remember what I used to be,
And dream of how I died.

You will see gloom and horror
But never the joy of fight.
You'll dream of me in pain and fear,
And in your dreaming never hear
My voice across the night.

My voice that sounds so gaily
Will be too far away
For you to see across your dream
The charging and the bayonet's gleam,
Or hear the words I say.

And parted by the warders
That hold the gates of sleep,
I shall be dead and happy
And you will live and weep.

THE LABYRINTH, *May* 15, 1916

IN MEMORIAM

Private D. Sutherland killed in Action in the German Trench, May 16, 1916, and the Others who Died.

SO you were David's father,
   And he was your only son,
And the new-cut peats are rotting
And the work is left undone,
Because of an old man weeping,
Just an old man in pain,
For David, his son David,
That will not come again.

Oh, the letters he wrote you,
And I can see them still,
Not a word of the fighting
But just the sheep on the hill
And how you should get the crops in
Ere the year got stormier,

You were, only David's father,
But I had fifty sons
When we went up in the evening
Under the arch of the guns,
And we came back at twilight—
O God ! I heard them call
To me for help and pity
That could not help at all.

Oh, never will I forget you,
My men that trusted me,
More my sons than your fathers',
For they could only see
The little helpless babies
And the young men in their pride.
They could not see you dying,
And hold you while you died.

Happy and young and gallant,
They saw their first-born go,

But not the strong limbs broken
And the beautiful men brought low,
The piteous writhing bodies,
The screamed, " Don't leave me, Sir,"
For they were only your fathers
But I was your officer.

A CREED

OUT of the womb of time and dust of the years forgotten,
    Spirit and fire enclosed in mutable flesh and bone,
Came by a road unknown the thing that is me for ever,
    The lonely soul of a man that stands by itself alone.

This is the right of my race, the heritage won by my fathers,
    Theirs by the years of fighting, theirs by the price they paid,
Making a son like them, careless of hell or heaven,
    A man that can look in the face of the gods and be not afraid.

Poor and weak is my strength and I cannot war against heaven,
    Strong, too strong are the gods ; but there is one thing that
      I can
Claim like a man unshamed, the full reward of my virtues,
    Pay like a man the price for the sins I sinned as a man.

Now is the time of trial, the end of the years of fighting,
    And the echoing gates roll back on the country I cannot see
If it be life that waits I shall live for ever unconquered,
    If death I shall die at last strong in my pride and free.

VIMY RIDGE, 1916

PEACE UPON EARTH

UNDER the sky of battle, under the arch of the guns,
   Where in a mad red torrent the river of fighting runs,
Where the shout of a strong man sounds no more than a broken
   groan,
And the heart of a man rejoicing stands up in its strength
   alone,
There in the hour of trial ; and when the battle is spent,
And we sit drinking together, laughing and well content,
Deep in my heart I am hearing a little still voice that sings,
" Well, but what will you do when there comes an end of these
   things ? "

Laughter, hard drinking and fighting, quarrels of friend and
   friend,
The eyes of the men that trust us, of all these there is an end.
No more in the raving barrage in one swift clamorous breath
We shall jest and curse together on the razor-edge of death.
Old days, old ways, old comrades, for ever and ever good-bye !

44

We shall walk no more in the twisted ways of the trenches, you
and I,

For the nations have heard the tidings, they have sworn that
wars shall cease,

And it's all one damned long Sunday walk down the straight,
flat road of peace.

Yes, we shall be raptured again by the frock-coat's singular
charm,

That goes so well with children and a loving wife on your arm,

Treading a road that is paved with family dinners and teas,

A sensible dull suburban road planted with decorous trees,

Till we come at last to the heaven our peaceable saints have
trod,

Like the sort of church that our fathers built and called it a
house of God,

And a God like a super-bishop in an apron and nice top-hat—

O God, you are God of battles.   Forbid that we come to that !

God, you are God of soldiers, merry and rough and kind,

Give to your sons an earth and a heaven more to our mind,

Meat and drink for the body, laughter and song for the soul,

And fighting and clean quick death to end and complete the
whole.

Never a hope of heaven, never a fear of hell,

Only the knowledge that you are a soldier, and all is well,

And whether the end be death or a merrier life be given,

We shall have died in the pride of our youth—and that will be
heaven.

On the road to Fricourt, 1916

THE VOLUNTEER

I TOOK my heart from the fire of love,
 Molten and warm not yet shaped clear,
And tempered it to steel of proof
 Upon the anvil-block of fear.

With steady hammer-strokes I made
 A weapon ready for the fight,
And fashioned like a dagger-blade
 Narrow and pitiless and bright.

Cleanly and tearlessly it slew,
 But as the heavy days went on
The fire that once had warmed it grew
 Duller, and presently was gone.

Oh, innocence and lost desire,
 I strive to kindle you in vain,
Dead embers of a greying fire.
 I cannot melt my heart again.

1914-1916

ON VIMY RIDGE

ON Vimy Ridge four months ago
    We lived and fought, my friends and I,
And watched the kindly dawn come slow,
Peace bringing from the eastern sky.
Now I sit in a quiet town
Remembering how I used to go
Among the dug-outs up and down,
On Vimy Ridge four months ago.

And often sitting here I've seen,
As then I saw them every night,
The friendly faces tired and keen
Across the flickering candle-light,
And heard their laughter gay and clear,
And watched the fires of courage glow
Above the scattered ash of fear,
On Vimy Ridge four months ago.

Oh, friends of mine, where are you now ?
Somewhere beneath the troubled sky,
With earth above the quiet brow,
Reader and Stalk for ever lie.
But dead or living out or here
I see the friends I used to know,
And hear the laughter gay and clear,
On Vimy Ridge four months ago.

IN MEMORIAM

R. M. Stalker   Missing, September 1916

As I go down the highway,
  And through the village street,
I hear the pipers playing
  And the tramp of marching feet.
The men I worked and fought with
  Swing by me four on four,
And at the end you follow
  Whom I shall see no more.

Oh, Stalk, where are you lying?
  Somewhere and far away,
Enemy hands have buried
  Your quiet contemptuous clay.
There was no greeting given,
  No tear of friend for friend,
From us when you flew over
  Exultant to the end.

I couldn't see the paper,
    I couldn't think that you
Would never walk the highway
    The way you used to do.
I turn at every footfall,
    Half-hoping, half-afraid
To see you coming, later
    Than usual for parade.

The old Lairg clique is broken,
    I drove there yesterday,
And the car was full of ghosts that sat
    Beside me all the way.
Ghosts of old songs and laughter,
    Ghosts of the jolly three,
That went the road together
    And go no more with me.

Oh, Stalk, but I am lonely,
    For the old days we knew,
And the bed on the floor at Lesdos
    We slept in, I and you.

The joyful nights in billets
   We laughed and drank and swore—
But the candle's burned out now, Stalk,
   In the mess at Henancourt.

The candle's burned out now, old man,
   And the dawn's come grey and cold,
And I sit by the fire here
   Alone and sad and old.
Though all the rest come back again,
   You lie in a foreign land,
And the strongest link of all the chain
   Is broken in my hand.

OTHER POEMS

THE KINGDOM OF THE DOWNS

BEYOND the woodland's shading,
   Beyond the sun-kissed field,
Where laughs in joy unfading
   The garden of the weald,
Look southward where uplifted
   Against the shining skies,
In secret vesture shifted,
   The silent Downs arise.

Until you see delusive
   Flash from the guardian down
A visioned land elusive,
   Dream of an unknown town,
And longing for the wonder,
   Strive what you dare not ask,
To rend the veil asunder
   And pluck away the mask.

Oh keep your spirit's vision
　　Although your eyes be blind,
Nor tempt the gods' derision
　　Of him that cannot find,
Lest you should lose the city
　　That once afar you saw,
And with it lose—ah, pity !—
　　All that was yours before.

Better dream on for ever
　　What once you dreamt was true,
Ere knowledge can dissever
　　Your visioned truth from you,
And from the wealden gazing
　　Watch how the sunset crowns
With dreamful beacons blazing
　　Your kingdom of the Downs.

In the Train, 1911

TO THE UNKNOWN LOVE

I CANNOT see you in the light
  Or find you in the day,
For when the sun springs up at dawn
  I think you slip away.

I wait until the night is come
  To pass beyond the veil,
And then I find you in the land
  Of the unuttered tale.

Then gazing out across the night
  I see with glad surmise
The shadows of your loosened hair,
  The depth of your grave eyes.

St Paul's, 1912

TO CATULLUS

A RONDEL

LAUGHTER and tears to you the gods once gave,
 Those silver tears upon your brother's grave,
And golden laughter in your lady's bower,
And silver-gold in your love's bitter hour.
You showed us, burdened with our hopes and fears,
  Laughter and tears.

Poor tears that fell upon the thirsty sands,
Poor laughter stifled with ungentle hands,
Poor heart that was so sweet to laugh and cry,
Your joyful, mournful songs shall never die,
But show us still across the shadowing years
  Laughter and tears.

St Paul's, 1912

58

MALLAIG BAY

I AM sickened of the south and the kindness of the downs,
  And the weald that is a garden all the day,
And I'm weary for the islands and the Scuir that always frowns,
  And the sun rising over Mallaig Bay.

I am sickened of the pleasant down and pleasant weald below,
  And the meadows where the little breezes play,
And I'm weary for rain-cloud over stormy Coolin's brow,
  And the wind blowing into Mallaig Bay.

I am sickened of the people that have ease in what they earn,
  The happy folk who have forgot to pray,
And I'm weary for the faces that are sorrowful and stern,
  And the boats coming into Mallaig Bay.

SUSSEX, 1912

VERSES TO TWO CHILDREN

DARLINGS, if I may call you so, ·
    I fear that I can only sing
Of sorrows that your elders know.
    To you I send a better thing.

Oh may you wander many a day
    Across the great Gromboolian plain,
Because, when I was far away,
    You came and brought me back again.

Because, when darkness covered me,
    You came and took me by the hand,
And opened my blind eyes to see
    The little hills of Fairyland.

BRORA, 1912

IN THE NIGHT

GALLANT fellows, tall and strong,
    Oh your strength was not for long,
Now within its bed alone
Quiet lies your nerveless bone.

Merry maidens young and fair,
Now your heads are bleached and bare,
Grinning mouths that smiled so sweet,
Buried deep the dancing feet.

Men and maidens fair and brave
Resting in your darkened grave,
Have you left the light behind,
Will you never feel the wind ?

Oh I know not if you may,
But from eve till dawn of day
Terror holds me in my bed,
Terror of the living dead.

OXFORD, 1912

CAROL OF THE INNOCENTS

AS I look out upon the sky
        And watch the clouds come driving by,
I know when for a moment's space
I see a laughing baby's face,
It is the Innocents that ride
Across the sky at Christmastide.

Above the world they dance and play,
And they are happy all the day,
And welcome on the joyous morn
A little king among them born.
God looks upon them as they go,
And laughs to see them frolic so.

Their little clouds are stained with red
To show how shamefully they bled,

CHRISTMAS, 1913

WANDERER'S DESIRE

To E. J. S. AND F. O. T.

I CANNOT sleep for thinking
    Of things that I have seen
About the highways of the world,
    Where fields are fresh and green,
And hedges lie on either hand
    With a white road between.

I cannot rest for dreaming
    Of places I have known,
The grasses of the lonely hills,
    The meadows and the sown,
And all the secrets which appear
    To men who walk alone.

The comrades of my walking
    Are calling me to go,

I cannot rise and follow

    The way they're calling me,

So I sit dreaming all the day,

    And all the day I see

The open highways of the world

    Where I would like to be.

OXFORD, 1913

GROWING PAINS

I

MY virtue is gone from me.   Nevermore
  Shall I see all the flowers and grasses plain,
But only sit and think how once I saw,
  And only pray that I may see again.
And in my ears all melody will die,
  And on my lips the songs I make will fade,
And I shall only hear in memory
  A far-off echo of the songs I made.
And the old happy vision of God's grace,
  Where I have mingled with eternal light,
Will comfort me no more, but in its place
  There will be darkness and eternal night;
And faintly in the darkness you will move,
And I shall keep the memory of love.

II

I cannot see your face, I cannot see
 The hair back-sweeping from your candid brow,
For night eternal overshadows me,
 And eyes that saw you once are sightless now
I cannot hear the music of your voice
 That was so beautiful while I could hear,
But only wait upon you and rejoice
 To know that in the darkness you are near.
Oh come to me, my dear, and loose my chain,
 And with your magic break the evil spell,
And bring me back into the light again
 To the fair country where I used to dwell.
For now my ears are deaf, my eyes are blind,
And endless darkness gathers in my mind.

III

The end has come for me, the end has come,
 The fairies have rung out their silver bell,
And after time will find and leave me dumb
 With no more tales of fairyland to tell.

The end has come for me, the end of all,
   Of song half-uttered and of quick desire,
And hopes that strained to heaven in their fall,
   And high dreams fashioned out of clay and fire.
The earth is black about me, and the sun
   Is blotted out with darkness overhead,
There is no hope to comfort me not one,
   For love has stolen away, and faith has fled,
And life that once was mine has passed me by,
And I am desolate and shall not die.

IV

There is a city built with walls of gold,
   Which is the birthplace of the fairy kings,
Full of strange songs and stories yet untold,
   And all the happiness that childhood brings.
The city's gates are open night and day,
   And night and day the travellers ride through,
And many that have wandered far away
   Would reach again the happy town they knew.
But they can only watch the vision die,
   And hear the music cease along the strand,

OXFORD, 1913

SONNET

EACH time we meet, my dear, I fancy you,
  A maiden both familiar and strange,
For still I see a girl I never knew

  And see my own dear love without a change;
And while young love is born within my heart,
  As on his birthday half a year ago,
I mourn that we are kept so long apart,
  And welcome joyfully the love I know.
As when a rover under foreign skies
  From some clear hill beholds a smiling plain,
And long-forgotten meadows meet his eyes,
  And memory awakens in his brain,
And suddenly he sees with glad surprise
  The open doorway of his home again.

OXFORD, 1913

TO ——

YOU have destroyed my early loves,
  The grasses wet with dew,
And hills upon whose gentle breast
  My careless boyhood grew.
I have no happiness at all
  Except to be with you.

I have forgotten all the words
  And laughter of my friends,
The little inns that are like homes,
  The road that dips and bends;
I hear them like a far-off song
  That fails at last and ends.

It's little use for us to grieve
  For things that cannot be;
You can't give back the happiness
  You took away from me.
Give me yourself, for night and day
  It's only you I see.

OXFORD, 1913

71

DEAD YOUTH

THE days of dreams are over,
  The days of songs are done,
So bid good-bye, young lover,
  To boyhood's dying sun;
Good-bye to joy and sadness,
  Good-bye to sun and rain,
And to the swift spring madness
  That will not come again.

Oh days of careless laughter,
  Oh nights of sudden tears,
We shall not know hereafter
  Forgotten hopes and fears.
Oh dreams that bide no longer
  With young hearts waxen cold,
Are lovely things no stronger,
  And must you too grow old?

Yes, memory is flying,
   And golden dreams must fade,
And all our loves are dying
   With us beneath the shade;
And buds that ripen never
   Their bloomless leaves have shed,
For youth is dead for ever,
   And all his thoughts are dead.

1913

AT THE END

IN the dim years, when earth's last sun is setting,
  And all the lamps of heaven are burning low,
Will the gods grant remembrance or forgetting
  Of joys and sorrows that possess us now ?

When the day ends and there is no to-morrow,
  Will there be thoughts alive to hurt us yet ?
Shall we remember, keeping all our sorrow,
  Or lose our little joys if we forget ?

Oh sure, since joy and pain we may not sever,
  Better it is to take the whole alloy,
And keep immortal grief, than lose for ever
  Our slight inheritance of immortal joy.

1913

ECCLESIASTES

OH vanity of vanities
    And following of wind
Through the dim avenues and deep
    Abysses of the mind;
When will our ears be deaf at last,
    When will our eyes be blind?

Oh vanity of vanities
    And lighter than the air,
And restless hearts unsatisfied
    With searching everywhere;
When will the restless heart be still,
    And loosened from its care?

Oh vanity of sorrowing
    And emptiness of mirth,

THE LOST LANDS

" OH where are the old kingdoms,
  Where is the ancient way,
And the remembered city
  Where once I used to play ? "
" You stand within the kingdom,
  You walk the city's street,
And still there throng about you
  The folk you used to meet."

" Where are the merry voices
  And laughter trouble-free,
And where are my old comrades
  That used to play with me ? "
" Their merry voices call you
  But you will not reply.
They touch your hand in welcome,
  But now you pass them by."

" Where is my love departed
　With her delightful eyes,
And heart too free for sorrow,
　And lips too proud for sighs ? "
" Along the road beside you
　Your true love walks and near,
But she may call for ever,
　And you will never hear."

OXFORD, 1915

CLYTEMNESTRA

OUT of the drinking cup,
   Out of my own hearth-fire,
The taint of blood goes up,
   The scent of the burning pyre.
When the feasters' shout is high,
   Or the spinning maidens sing,
I hear the dead man's cry,
   The dead who was my king.

For this is an ageless thing,
   And the blood runs fresh again
In the cleansing draught from the spring
   And the storèd wine I drain.
And the joyous marriage-song,
   And the drinking-song at the board,
Is the voice that sobbed so long
   In the agony of my lord.

Oh dark stern face of him
    I wedded and could not love,
Oh terrible eyes grown dim
    And torn black hair above,
Oh hands so strong in fight,
    So weak in the folding net,
Dead feet that by day and night
    Follow the slayer yet,

Lo I am drawing near
    To the door of the house of death,
Must I for ever hear
    The sound of the labouring breath,
Must I for ever see
    The murdered body lie,
And on my own roof-tree
    The blood that will not dry ?

1914

DEDICATION

IF in my song the heart of love
   Looks from another maiden's eyes,
Where on the hills of Morven move
   The kings too proud for Paradise,
Though to your ears the autumn brings
   No sounds of crying, you will know
The murmur of immortal things
   In this dark tale of long ago.

If in the silence of the nights
   The song of Angus calls no more,
If all the sea is ringed with lights
   And no waves moaning on the shore.
Though Balor sleeping on the hills
   Forgets the dew in his drenched hair,
You will remember ancient ills
   Pitying another Alastair.

F

81

THREE SONGS FROM THE
REMEMBERED GODS

ANGUS' SONG

ARE the gods forgotten in Morven of the hinds,
    The beauty that slew men the golden eyes that shone
The gods that will bé walking on the rocks of the winds
    That little men would die for the love of looking on ?

Are the gods forgotten in Morven of the stags,
    The old gods, the fair gods that were too high for love,
The white feet pressing on the grasses of the crags,
    The black hair hidden in the black clouds above ?

The gods are forgotten in Morven of the glens,
    The sun shines brightly and gentle is the day.
Like snow in summer corries, like mist upon the bens,
    The lovely gods of darkness are vanished away.

ALASTAIR'S SONG

Summer is gone at last and autumn leaves are falling,
   And through the naked trees the wind is breathing low.
Let us arise and go for the old gods are calling,
   The beautiful cruel gods we loved so long ago.

Let us arise and go, for far beyond the city
   We hear the old gods singing the years from which we came.
The merry heartless years that knew not pain or pity,
   The happy lustful years that knew not fear or shame.

The bitter music calls, and we must follow after,
   Back through the gentler years to the old time again.
To wake their lovely mirth, to move the gods to laughter,
   This is the end of man, the full reward of pain.

The golden eyes aglow, the silver laughter ringing,
   Shall we not suffer pain for lovely things as these ?
Let us arise and go, for the old gods are singing,
   The beautiful cruel gods that mock our miseries.

THE MEMORY SONG

Long ago beneath the moon
In a corrie of the hills
We forgot our ancient ills
Dancing to a wizard tune.
We remembered song and spell
Chanted in a Lochlainn rune,
Flower of Morven, it was well
Long ago beneath the moon.

Now the moon is full again,
And the song of Angus cries
Underneath the summer skies
Till the nights of summer wane.
Follow now while still you may,
Ere his music calls in vain,
When the harps of Angus play
Now the moon is full again.

Flower of Morven, long ago
In the corrie where we met,
Did you think you could forget,
Did you dream you would not know

Oh, remember me once more,
Now the mist is on the hills
And the harp of Angus thrills
Moaning waves along the shore,
For the songs I made for you,
For the love that was before,
For the heart that still is true,
Oh, remember me once more.

NEIL'S SONG

From " THE LATER WOOING "

NOW the day is growing old
  And the shadows pace
Slower now, and now more cold
  O'er the water's face.
When my heart is ebbing low
  With the ebbing tide,
When the happy visions go,
  Why should life abide ?

Now with whispers from the sea
  The little winds go by
Moaning, moaning hopelessly
  That the day should die.
When the hours of memory fill
  All my heart with pain,
When my dreams go down the hill
  Why should life remain ?

Now the world is burning out
    Mountain, glen and sea.
From their barrows all about
    The dead are calling me.
When my hope is flown and dead
    With my love of you,
When the heart of life is fled,
    Shall not life go too ?

1914

OLD AGE

IN the old years that creep on us so fast,
  When Time goes by us with a halting tread,
Shall we sit still and ponder at the last
  The young swift years of love that will be dead ?
Shall we look back upon the passionate years,
  Where in a maze our younger figures move,
Instinct with half-forgotten hopes and fears,
  And gaze anew on the mirage of love ?

Yes, we two, like old actors at the play,
  Watching the beating of a tinsel heart,
Will laugh and weep, and clap our hands, and say,
  " How sadly that young lover played his part
That loved her true and dared not tell her so,
  And she that loved him dared not let him see,"
And we shall watch the hurts of long ago,
  And clap our hands at our old tragedy.

For we shall understand, remembering
   How he spoke thus and she would answer so,
And then we shall see clearly everything
   That was so dark in youth's old puppet-show,
And gazing on the far-off stage where stand
   The misty figures that were you and I,
Each in the darkness will stretch out a hand
   To touch the hand of love before we die.

OXFORD, 1914

THE HEARTLESS VOICE

YOUR voice is like the fairy harps
    The wandering shepherd hears,
That tell of laughter without joy,
    And light unsaddened tears.

You laugh and I can never tell
    If you are glad or no,
You weep and cannot understand
    The things that hurt me so.

But still your eager, heartless voice
    Is calling night and day,
And I must follow like the men
    That hear the fairies play.

1914

HOPE

WHERE is the life of springs forgotten.
The happy life of years grown old?
Their bloomless buds are dead and rotten,
The suns that warmed their leaves are cold.
And we that walk the ruined garden
Watch the dry breath of winter harden
In all its beds the barren mould.

Where is the joy of daily meeting
In spring-time when the sun was high?
The winter suns are pale and fleeting,
The gathering clouds o'ercast the sky.
And we that walk alone remember
The fires whose last undying ember
Will burn our hearts until we die.

Oh, heart of youth, too full of sorrow,
Be strong and hold your sorrow fast.

There where the flowers and grasses cover
The lips that laugh, the eyes that weep,
Lover shall meet again with lover,
No man shall break the tryst they keep.
You shall fulfil desire with dreaming
There where all life is inward seeming,
There where the heart of life is sleep.

1914

THE LAST MEETING

L AST time you met me shadowed white,
  A very queen for stateliness,
And all the jewels of the night
  Were tangled in your ivory dress.
Your eyes were strange, your lovely smile
  As though we never met before—
I saw you such a little while,
  Who shall not see you evermore.

God knows the gates were strong between,
  But still my trumpet might have blown
Had you not looked so great a queen,
  Had I but seen you all alone.
But there we sat the dinner through
  And talked like strangers of the war.
  only spoke an hour with you,
  Who now shall speak with you no more.

Maybe I waited over-long,
    You spoke no word to tell me so.
Perhaps the gates might be too strong
    For any blast that I could blow—
Ah well, it hardly matters now,
    My whispering ghost drifts through the rain,
The shroud of death is at my brow,
    I shall not come to you again.

1915

VALE ATQUE AVE

IS it good-bye for ever
  For us beneath the sun ?
The lads and girls go over,
With every girl a lover,
And never a lonely one,
But I shall see you never
Till all my days are done.

I could not read your letter,
I could not think it true,
Seeing the lands and hedges
And the long naked ridges
And skies serene and blue.
Though worse should come or better
I walk no more with you.

And I saw the winter weather
And the joyous days of spring.

Love is not dead but sleeping,
Youth is not spent in vain.
Another hand will hold me,
And other arms enfold me,
To feel in every vein
The blood of youth go leaping ;
But you come not again.

You've gone, and with you flying
The grace of life is past,
And I go robbed and wanting
Till with a little panting
My labouring life ebbs fast,
And I look up in dying
And see you at the last.